QUALITIES OF
A DEVOTED SOUL

A Portrayal of the Hizmet People

From soulmate to soulmate...

"The bond between believers is like the bond between the components which keep the building together..." – Hadith

Read this book.
Feel it in your soul.

Then just like Aisha (RA)
be a fountain of knowledge
for everyone.
Witness truth.
Overflow with kindness.
Pump the love you feel
in your heart to others...

Peace ♡
↑
I'm a terrible artist.

QUALITIES OF A DEVOTED SOUL

A Portrayal of the Hizmet People

İbrahim Özübüyük

TUGHRA
BOOKS

New Jersey

Originally published in Turkish as *Adanmışların Vasıfları* in 2010

16 15 14 13   1 2 3 4

Published by Tughra Books
345 Clifton Ave., Clifton,
NJ, 07011, USA

www.tughrabooks.com

Library of Congress Cataloging-in-Publication Data Available

ISBN: 978-1-59784-292-1

Translated by Ömer A. Ergi

Printed by
Görsel Dizayn Ofset., İstanbul - Turkey

Contents

1

THE SENTIMENT OF RESPONSIBILITY AND SERVING RELIGION

Taking a step on the path to pleasing God with an intention to strive in God's cause and for humanity's good is more blessed than everything in the world.[1]

What Do the Words "Being Conscious of Your Responsibility" Mean?

Scholars have defined responsibility as one's accountability and liability towards certain obligations such as belief, practice, behavior, action and speech. In fact, being cognizant of responsibilities is one of the most significant qualities that distinguish human beings from the animals, because, a human being is a living entity who possesses intellect, freewill, responsibility and faith.

A believer is a person of responsibility. He or she has a responsibility towards God, the noble Prophet and all Muslims. Sometimes this responsibility manifests itself as making an effort on the path of God and sometimes as good manners.

All Muslims are obligated to keep their promise to God and behave in a manner of being aware of their responsibilities. So what was this promise we made to God? If we contemplate on the promise we made to God in regard to Him being our Lord,[2] and about the reason of our creation which is worship and servanthood, we would

---

[1] *Sahih al-Bukhari*, Jihad, 5
[2] Al-A'raf 7:172

have a better understanding of our responsibilities. Our Lord explains this with the following verse: *"God burdens no soul except within its capacity: in its favor is whatever (good) it earns, and against it whatever (evil) it merits"* (al-Baqarah 2:286).

An individual who is aware of his responsibilities will never forget this verse hence act accordingly. As this verse carries a severe caution for people of responsibility who wish to serve their religion, it also explains an important decree: A human being is accountable towards things he is able to carry.

Without doubt, faith is the greatest blessing God has bestowed upon His servants. True gratitude for the gift of faith can only be displayed by taking this blessing to souls who are in need of it. This aspiration and feeling is the biggest responsibility of a believer. This noble duty which was exemplified by the Companions of the Prophet at one time, have now been placed on the shoulders of the believers of today as a blessing from God. Of course, taking on the role of the Companions is a difficult task but it is also a most noble duty.

A believer who is aware of his responsibility is a person whose backbone crunches under the heavy load of servanthood and lives his life in two-folds within the comprehension of the meaning of worship. For this reason, our noble Prophet states: "If you knew what I know, you would have wept a lot and laughed a lot less."[3] The noble Prophet was groaning under the weight of servanthood and responsibility. How about us? How conscious are we of our responsibilities?

We must never forget, as described beautifully by Fethullah Gülen Hocaefendi (pronounced as "Hodjaefendi," an honorific meaning "respected teacher"), "We are charged with the responsibility for endowing our world with a fresh, new spirit, woven from a love of faith, a love of our fellow human being, and a love of freedom. We have further been charged with the responsibility for being ourselves, connected to the principle of these three loves, and for preparing the ground for the shoots, the pure roots of the blessed tree of Paradise, so that it will be nurtured and grow in the loam of these loves. This,

---

[3]   *Sahih al-Bukhari*, Kusuf, 2

of course, depends on the existence of heroes who will take responsibility for and protect the country's destiny and the history, religion, traditions, culture, and all sacred things that belong to the people; this will depend on heroes who are absolutely full of a love for science and knowledge, burgeoning with the thought of improvement and construction, sincere and devout beyond measure, patriotic and responsible, and, therefore, always conscientiously at work, in charge, and on duty.

Thanks to these heroes and their sincere efforts, our system of thoughts and understanding and the fruit of these will prevail with our people; the sense of devoting oneself to others and to the community will gain prominence; the understanding of the division of labor, the management of time, and assisting and liaising with one another will be revived; all relationships of authority-subject, employer-employee, landlord-tenant, landowner-peasant, artist-admirer, attorney-client, teacher-student will become different aspects of the unity of the whole; all this will come about once more and all our expectations from ages past will come true, one by one. We now live in an era in which our dreams are being realized and we believe that with good timing each of the responsibilities of the age will have been accomplished by the time its day arrives."[4]

Consequently, we should leave comforts and worldly pleasures aside, purify ourselves from satanic thoughts like "who cares" and fulfill our responsibilities.

The Feeling of Responsibility Demonstrated by the Prophet and His Companions

Our noble Prophet felt the weight of responsibility so extensively that when the Surah Hud was revealed, the number of grays on his blessed beard had increased drastically. They asked him:

"O Messenger of God, lately, the grays on your beard have increased significantly."

---

[4]   Gülen, M. Fethullah, *The Statue of Our Souls*, New Jersey: Tughra Books, 2009, pp. 101–102

He replied: "Surah Hud has aged me."

Once again, they asked: "Which verse, O Messenger of God?"

He replied: *"Pursue, then, what is exactly right (in every matter of the Religion), as you are commanded (by God)"* (Hud 11:112).

In every level of his invitation to religion, the noble Messenger, a man of greatest responsibility, always emphasized the significance of the sentiment of responsibility to the people he addressed, because, people who possess a sense of responsibility will always behave in a shrewd and appropriate manner. At times, our Prophet mentioned that all Muslims have responsibilities and at times he indicated to a certain group as he talked about human responsibilities. There were also occasions where he reminded one person of his responsibilities. Let us now provide some examples in regard to this topic.

Our Prophet indicated that every individual in society has responsibilities and he exempted no one: "You are all shepherds and you are all responsible of those under your hand. A leader of a nation is a shepherd and those under his rule are his responsibility. Every individual is a shepherd of his family thus he is responsible for them. A woman is the shepherd of her husband's home and she is responsible of its supervision. A servant is responsible for his master's belongings therefore he is also a shepherd. Each and every one of you is a shepherd and you are responsible of those under your rule."[5]

In relation to inviting people to the universal virtues, every Muslim is held responsible. "Whoever sees an evil let him correct it with his hands. If he does not have the power to do this let him correct it with his tongue. If he does not possess the strength to do this also, then let him display his repugnance with his heart."[6] (When practicing this *hadith*, Muslims should not violate the laws of their host country.)

Our Prophet gave great importance to knowledge, learning and teaching. He focused on responsibility before action. His cautions about responsibility continued during also during practice. According

---

[5]   *Sahih al-Bukhari*, Jumua, 11; *Sahih Muslim*, Imarat, 20; *Sunan Abu Dawud*, Haraj, 1
[6]   *Sahih Muslim*, Iman, 87

to the noble Prophet this was a progression that did not conclude at a certain point. The reason for this was that the society of that era did not have a solid structure; it was always going through a change. The number of individuals in the community constantly increased, so it was imperative that essential information be repeated for those who recently joined the community.

Our Prophet has many statements which describe the different aspects of responsibility. It is obvious that if a movement is disciplined through the sentiment of responsibility, it will be more beneficial. In contrast, movements not disciplined through the sense of responsibility will beget anarchy and chaos. The Messenger of God has developed the character of those around him through the sentiment of responsibility and transformed them into individuals who were beneficial to society. The sentiment of responsibility preached by the noble Prophet can be seen in the lives and behavior of the Companions.

Our Prophet used to assign responsibilities to his Companions in regard to conveying the truth. One of these Companions was Mus'ab ibn Umayr. He was the son of a wealthy Meccan family. Mus'ab was a gentle, civilized and a handsome young man. He turned his back to all the wealth that his family possessed to become a Muslim. Following the first pledge at Aqaba, our Prophet sent Mus'ab to Medina to teach Islam and the recitation of the Qur'an to those who had accepted his Prophethood. In Medina, Mus'ab stayed in the home of Asad ibn Zurara.

Mus'ab, a man of responsibility who exerted all of his efforts to explain Islam was being guided by Asad ibn Zurara who took him to the leaders of Medina. Many people in Medina had already embraced Islam. However, this needed to be done on a larger scale thus meetings with the leaders were imperative. It was important to encourage some of the prominent leaders to embrace Islam.

Sa'd ibn Muaz, the leader of the Aws tribe was not Muslim yet and he was concerned about the spread of Islam in Medina. He sent Usayd ibn Khudayr, who was also one of the leaders of his tribe, to Mus'ab so that he could stop him from spreading Islam. He also added, "I know what to do with him, if only my cousin Asad ibn Zurara was not involved."

Usayd rushed to the location where Mus'ab had gathered with a small group of people. Usayd was furious as he approached the group. Asad had noticed the approach of Usayd and quickly turned to Mus'ab and explained that he was one of the leaders of their tribe. Usayd stood next to them and shouted, "Why have you come here! You are misleading some of our weak and ignorant people. If you don't want to lose your life, leave at once!"

Mus'ab replied, "Wait, come and sit down for a moment. Listen to what I am saying. If you agree with what I am saying then you will accept; if you don't then you may do as you wish with me." This was a kind and friendly reply by Mus'ab.

Usayd said, "You have spoken the truth." He then placed his spear on the ground and sat next to them. Mus'ab explained Islam to him and then recited a few verses from the Holy Qur'an. Usayd could not hold himself anymore as he said, "What beautiful words are these? How does one embrace this religion?" Mus'ab and Asad explained that first he needed to wash up, change his clothes and then recite the testimony of faith. They also added that he should perform the Prayer. Usayd followed all the instructions and became a Muslim. Later, he stood up and said, "I will go now and send someone important to you. If this man embraces Islam, there will be no one left in this region to decline this religion."

Quickly, he went back to Sa'd ibn Muaz. Sa'd asked, "What have you done with them?" He replied, "I did what was necessary and spoke to them but I did not see any problems with those two." Sa'd said, "Your explanation is not satisfactory."

Sa'd became extremely upset as he decided to solve the problem himself. He took off and quickly found Mus'ab and Asad. He shouted in anger as he stood over them, "O Asad! If we were not related, I would not have shown any tolerance towards you, for you have brought disorder into our people!"

Upon hearing this, Mus'ab replied in a gentle manner, "Please sit with us for a moment. Listen to what I am saying. If you find these words acceptable then embrace them. If you find them to be repulsive then we will stop conveying them."

Sa'd was convinced as he sat down and listened. Mus'ab explained the meaning of Islam and recited a few verses from the Holy Qur'an. As he recited the verses, Sa'd's expression changed and signs of faith began to appear on his face. Suddenly, he said, "What do you do to enter this religion?" Mus'ab explained the essentials of Islam and its values. Without hesitation Sa'd recited the testimony of faith and embraced Islam. Through Mus'ab's gentle attitude and sincere approach, there was not a house in Medina where Islam had not entered.[7] The Mus'ab-like people of today could learn a lot from these incidents.

The Spirit of Responsibility Should Always Be Kept Alive

When people utter the words "Why should I bother with this", a dialogue that took place between Sultan Süleyman the Magnificent and Yahya Efendi, who was an important scholar of the era, comes to mind. The Sultan and Yahya Efendi are milk-brothers. Yahya Efendi is a saintly individual whose prayers were potent.

One day, Sultan Süleyman ponders about the future of the Ottoman State and writes a letter to Yahya Efendi: "My dear brother, you are a scholar of wisdom. Bless us with your knowledge and tell us what will become of the sons of Uthman."

Yahya Efendi replies with the following message: "Why should I bother with this, brother?"

Sultan Süleyman was stunned by the reply hence quickly he decided to visit Yahya Efendi at his dervish lodge in Yıldız Park. He was disappointed at the fact that no answer was given to his question. As the Sultan walked in he asked, "Dear brother, you have not answered my question, have I done something wrong?"

Yahya Efendi replied, "I have answered your question, yet I am surprised that you failed to understand."

"What did it mean?" asked Sultan Süleyman.

---

[7] Ibn Hisham, *As-Sirah*, 1/275–277

Yahya Efendi replied: "My brother, in a nation, if injustice and tyranny becomes wide-spread and if those who see this say "Why should I bother with this" and do not act; if a sheep is consumed by the shepherd instead of a wolf and if those who know do not say anything; if the screams of the poor and the innocents rise to the sky and if no one hears them, then wait for the demise of you nation. Your treasures will be looted and your soldiers will rebel, this is the time of the end."

Fortunate are those who are aware of their humanity and possess exalted feelings of responsibility. They could never say, "Why should I bother with this." When they behold a bleeding wound, they do not ignore this as their hearts burn with agony. They feel ashamed before God and their conscience feel the pressure of the Prophet's spirituality hence they do not leave unguarded the sanctified cause which was entrusted upon them.[8]

READING TEXT

We Have Also Accepted the Resignation of Those Who Have Given Their Resignation to You!

Great poet Mehmet Akif Ersoy would frequently attend the Sultan Ahmed Mosque for the Morning Prayers. Each time he went to the mosque, he saw an old man weeping in the corner. One day, the old man explained his story to Akif and he was deeply affected. Later, Akif explained the conversation he had with the old man:

"Every day I would perform the Morning Prayer at Sultan Ahmed. No matter how early I went there, I would see an old man sitting at the corner of the Mosque and weeping continuously. His hair and beard had completely turned gray and the old man looked extremely sad and hopeless. He cried so much that I did not witness a minute in which he did not weep. I could not help myself but wonder as to why this man wept so much. One morning, I approached him and asked, "Why are you weeping so much? Should a man lose hope from the mercy of God?" He glanced at me with his aged eyes and replied:

---

[8] Akar, Mehmet, *Mesel Ufku*, İstanbul: Timaş, 2008, p. 104

"Do not make me explain. My heart is about to explode." I continued to insist and finally he began to explain his story: "Dear sir, I was a major in the army during the rule of Sultan Abdülhamid. I had a military unit under my command. I served in the army until my parents passed away. Following their deaths, I decided to resign from active duty. I had inherited a significant amount of wealth. In order to supervise this wealth, so that it was not misused, I decided to give in my resignation. I wrote a request for my resignation and sent it to the royal authority. In my request letter I had written, "Both my parents have passed away. We have a significant amount of wealth and properties at various locations. Consequently, someone needs to attend to our businesses and properties. Please consider my situation when deciding on my resignation."

A few days later, I received a letter from the Sultan himself. I opened the letter with great enthusiasm. The Sultan was informing me that my resignation was not accepted. It was obvious that they had given my resignation request letter to the Sultan himself. I wrote another letter and reapplied for it. There was no change in the decision. Finally, I decided to visit the Sultan in person and ask for my resignation. Sultan Abdülhamid was a courageous individual. Sometime ago, I worked with his personal assistant. He explained a few things about the Sultan: "When Abdülhamid traveled in his carriage, people sitting on his left and right would be afraid to even breathe."

Abdülhamid was a saintly person. For this reason, I decided to explain my situation to this majestic and heroic man in person, may God have mercy on his soul. I visited him and said:

"O Sire, I urge you to accept my resignation, this is my situation." He paused for a few minutes. I could tell from his expression that he did not wish to accept my resignation. For this reason I became a bit more adamant. Upon my persistence, he turned towards me and with anger he said "Your resignation has been accepted" as he made a push-away gesture with the back of his hand.

I was happy about the result. Quickly, I returned to my town and took control over my businesses. One night, I saw an incredible dream. In the realm of metaphysics all the Muslim armies had gathered for inspection. Our regiments fighting in the east and the west were being inspected by the Messenger of God, himself.

Our noble Prophet was standing in front of the Yıldız Palace and the entire army was marching through in total discipline as they saluted him. There were prominent Ottoman Sultans besides him and Abdülhamid was also there. The Sultan was standing behind the Prophet in a respectful manner. As the army marched through, the regiment that I used to command appeared. It did not have a commander hence the soldiers were walking in an undisciplined manner.

Upon seeing this, the noble Prophet turned to Abdülhamid and said: "O Abdülhamid, where is the commander of this regiment?"

Abdülhamid replied in humility: "O Messenger of God, the commander of this regiment resigned. He insisted so much that we gave him the permission to resign."

The noble Prophet said: "We have also accepted the resignation of those who have given their resignation to you!"

The old man concluded his story with the words, "Now tell me, should I stop crying or not?"

Indeed, the noble Prophet is behind every step that is taken in the name of God. If a believer wishes to see the Prophet's support then he should fulfill his duty accordingly.

What Should a Believer Be Careful of When Serving the Religion and his Nation?

What type of foundation should a responsible believer, whose heart beats with the passion for serving his religion and nation, possess? Let us now attempt to find an answer to this question.

First of all, we need to learn our religion appropriately. In order to do this, we need to learn the essentials of religion by studying from authentic sources. The knowledge learned should be reflected to our lives. Primarily, a person of responsibility must learn his religion within the framework of Sunni way of belief (*Ahl al-Sunnah wa al-Jama'a*) and accordingly put this knowledge into practice.

It is also important to show patience. As it is the case with all matters, our guide in conveying the truth to others is Prophet Muhammad, peace and blessings be upon him. When we analyze his luminous life, we see that he possessed the utmost patience.

As it is common knowledge, the greatest problems and hardships came to Prophets who were the most beloved servants of God, yet, they displayed great patience. No doubt, there may be obstacles of all kinds on the path of believers who wish to serve their religion and nation. They need to overcome these obstacles with great patience, like the patience we observe in the life of the noble Prophet.

The Messenger of God endured harassments of all types as thorns were laid on his path and intestines were poured over his head when he offered his Prayer. In spite of all, he showed incredible dedication, visiting every tent and every street in Mecca to guide people onto the right path.

One of the most important cornerstones in our Prophet's invitation is tolerance and gentleness. The Holy Qur'an describes our Prophet's gentle approach to people with the following verse:

> It was by a mercy from God that (at the time of the setback), you (O Messenger) were lenient with them (your Companions). Had you been harsh and hard-hearted, they would surely have scattered away from about you. Then pardon them, pray for their forgiveness, and take counsel with them in the affairs (of public concern); and when you are resolved (on a course of action), put your trust in God. Surely God loves those who put their trust (in Him). (Al Imran 3:159)

Benevolence is a radiant key granted to our Prophet for opening the tarnished hearts. With this key he has unlocked many hearts. Therefore, we should also equip ourselves with the following principles: "Be so tolerant that your heart becomes wide like the, ocean. Become inspired with faith and love for others. Offer a hand to those in trouble, and be concerned about everyone. Applaud the good for their goodness, appreciate those who have believing hearts, and be kind to believers. Approach unbelievers so gently that their envy and hatred. Return good for evil, and disregard discourteous treatment.

An individual's character is reflected in his or her behavior. Choose tolerance, and be magnanimous toward the ill-mannered. The most distinctive feature of a soul overflowing with faith is to love all types of love that are expressed in deeds, and to feel enmity for all deeds in which enmity is expressed. To hate everything is a sign of insanity or of infatuation with Satan."⁹

Another matter of utmost importance: We observe that in explaining Islam, the noble Prophet preferred to use a step by step method. If you place a fifty kilo load on a person whose capability is limited to twenty kilos, you will likely to cause an injury. The Messenger of God treated people according to their levels and ability, explaining the realities of religion not at once but in limited dosages with love and care hence this is how he enabled faith and virtues to enter their hearts.

We should also underline the following matter: A believer should fulfill his duty within the limits of causes however he should leave the result to God. In situations of success, one should never feel pride and vanity. On the contrary, one should always possess the thought that it is God who grants everything and nothing can be achieved without His help.

Finally, one should always take great care with his/her life of servanthood; alongside the Daily Prayers, there should be Tahajjud, Nafila, Awwabin, and also Tasbihat and Jawshan. They should never be neglected. One's daily life should be established on *taqwa* (the conscious performance of good and avoidance of evil) and *zuhd* (asceticism).

Grab Those Sticks, We Deserve This Punishment

In schools, moral and cultural values should be taught as much as the other subjects so that generations with powerful characters and strong spirits who would transform their nation into paradise can be raised. Teaching and nurturing are different things. Many people can be teachers but not everyone can be educators. Becoming a teacher-educator

---

⁹ Gülen, M. Fethullah, *Pearls of Wisdom*, New Jersey: Tughra Books, 2012, p. 75

depends on feeling the pressure of responsibility at all times and being two-folded with concerns and distress. Affecting the hearts of your pupils can only be achieved through the level of representation stated above. Here is an exemplary incident:

Nevzat hodja came to Haydar hodja in panic, "They ran away again. Many times we spoke to them and gave advice yet they did it again. They do not listen. This is the third time they took off."

Haydar hodja asked, "Why are they doing this?"

"I do not know; they want to live like fools," he replied.

"How did you find them last time?"

"The first time, we found them at the bus terminal and the second time they ran away we found them sleeping on a park bench. It was during the time of military restriction so soldiers found them and notified us. We went and brought them back. We explained to them that this kind of behavior would be costly, yet they do not understand."

Meanwhile, the three students who ran away had decided to purchase train tickets. The experienced conductor at the train station quickly realized that these kids were runaways. He said to them, "Listen kids, it is not safe around here, give me your tickets and money for safe-keeping. When the train arrives, I will give them back." The kids found this quite reasonable and gave their tickets to the conductor. The conductor then informed the police at the train station and asked them to investigate the kids. The policeman treated them kindly and asked about their situations. He found the name of the boarding school they had ran away from. Quickly he called their school and Haydar hodja jumped in the car and came to the station. He picked the three runaways up and brought them back to school. This time he was going to punish them severely, because they had been warned many times before. Upon arrival, he saw the principal and changed his mind about punishing the students. Then he explained the situation to him. The principal said, "Find me three steel rods and make sure they are thick, I do not want them to bend when I am thumping these three. I have a class now, bring them to me after I finish."

Haydar hodja walked out thinking, "Isn't one steel rod enough? It is not as if it would break like a stick." Then he argued in his mind, "I should be respectful, there must be some wisdom in this."

A few minutes later, he came back holding three steel rods in his hand. The principle had finished his class as the three students waited at the doorway like patients waiting for surgery, with fear on their eyes. The principle turned towards them and said, "Come on in." Then he turned to Haydar hodja and said, "Come on Haydar hodja take your shirt off, for I am doing the same." Then he looked at the three students and said, "Here take these steel rods! We deserved this punishment. If we were good examples and role models, if we had touched your hearts, you would not be doing this foolish thing. It is us who deserve this beating. Our backs are open, hit as much as you wish."

The three students who entered the room with pale faces and great fear were now in shock. The steel rods had fallen from their hands and they were on the floor, weeping. They pleaded to the principle, "Please sir, 'Punish us as you wish, break our legs but forgive us.'" The principle was quite serious in his decision to punish himself. However, the sincerity of the students had convinced him. Finally, he changed his mind and decided not to insist anymore. No one ran away from this boarding school again.[10]

Qualities of a Hizmet (Service) Devotee

In one of his articles, Fethullah Gülen summarizes the qualities of the people who have devoted themselves to Hizmet (a word of Arabic origin, used in Turkish to mean disinterested, voluntary and beneficial service to others):

1. People of service must resolve, for the sake of the cause to which they have given their heart, to cross over seas of "pus and blood."

2. When they attain the desired object, they must be mature enough to attribute everything to its Rightful Owner, and be

---

[10] Refik, İbrahim, *Hayatın Renkleri*, İstanbul: Albatros, 2001, p. 154

respectful and thankful to Him. Their voices and breaths glorify and magnify God, the Sublime Creator. Such people hold everyone in high regard and esteem, and are so balanced and faithful to God's Will that they do not idolize those whom they praise for their services.

3. First of all, they understand that they are responsible and answerable for work left undone, must be considerate and fair-minded to everyone who seeks their help, and must work to support the truth.

4. They are extraordinarily resolved and hopeful even when their institutions are destroyed, their plans upset, and their forces routed.

5. People of service are moderate and tolerant when they take new wings and once again soar to the summits, and so rational and wise that they admit in advance that the path is very steep. So zealous, persevering, and confident are they that they willingly pass through all the pits of hell encountered on the way.

6. So sincere and humble are such people that they never remind others of their accomplishments.[11]

It Cannot Be Achieved without Hardship and Suffering

One of the qualities of believers who consider serving religion as the objective of life is hardship and suffering. As it is known, the purpose of Prophets is to guide human beings onto the right path through invitation and supervision. There was not a moment in their lives in which this Divine mission did not take place. The most apparent activities observed in the lives of Prophets were reminding people about faith when they were amongst them; planning and producing strategies to fulfill this Divine mission when they were alone; asking help from God for success; praying and pleading for the salvation of those who detach themselves from God and experiencing hardship and suffering on this path.

---

[11] Gülen, M. Fethullah, *Pearls of Wisdom*, New Jersey: Tughra Books, 2012, pp. 103–104

Obviously, our noble Prophet was no different. He had great concern and affection for his people. He endured many difficulties and all forms of suffering so that people may embrace Islam. The Holy Qur'an explains his situation with the following verse: *"Now hath come unto you a Messenger from amongst yourselves: it grieves him that ye should perish: ardently anxious is he over you: to the Believers he is most kind and merciful"* (at-Tawbah 9:128).

Just as he did on earth, our noble Prophet will also make an effort to save the believers on the Day of Judgment by using his rights of intercession as he will appeal to the mercy of God for the salvation of those who are worthy of forgiveness. In this day and age, a Muslim should be sensitive about the situations of others, just like the Messenger of God, they should wish for them to have faith, learn the universal virtues and practice them accordingly so that they could achieve happiness in both worlds. Moreover, praying for their salvation and being concerned about their future is a Prophetic manner. For this reason, every soul that has possessed this responsibility has made it a habit to recite the following prayer: *"Allahummarham ummata Muhammad"*, O God, have mercy on the people of Muhammad, peace and blessings be upon him.

As explained above, this prayer includes a glimpse into the exalted perspective of the Prophets as it also shares their dignified views. People who possess such venerable ideals had sometimes stated, "O God, on the Day of Judgment, make my body so huge that it fills the entire Hell, this way there will be no room left for others!" There are also those who said: "I have sacrificed my world and the Hereafter for my people's faith. I am willing to smolder in the flames of hell if only I could see the salvation of my people's faith." Such people have displayed this act of self-sacrifice by continuously living in this frame of mind.

Let us try to strengthen our argument with an analogy: Once upon a time, a man thought to himself, "I wonder if there are saintly people in this day and age?" Suddenly he heard a voice, "Yes there is a person. He is a steelworker at such and such place and his name is Ahmad Efendi."

So this person searched for Ahmad Efendi and found him. From a distance he observed his lifestyle. He wanted to see the extraordinary qualities that Ahmad Efendi possessed. However, he could not see anything different about him.

Finally, he decided to visit him and tell him about his experience. Upon listening, Ahmad Efendi replied: "As you see, I do not have an intense religious life. I do not stay awake every night and I do not fast every day. However, when I place my steel on the fire and it turns red, and becomes ready for me to work on, the people of Muhammad, peace and blessings be upon him, come to my mind. I think about how they live detached from God and accompanied by sins. This is when I make the prayer, "O God, forgive Muslims and have mercy on them. Save them from this disgraceful situation." I lose myself in these thoughts so much so that sometimes I grab the steel from the hot side and I do not even feel the heat in my hand. The other person replied, "Ok, now I know why you are so valuable by the side of God."

Indeed, an individual who has dedicated himself to service must feel the pain and anguish of those who needs guidance. Following the death of Abu Ali Dakkak, a beloved servant of God, they see him in a dream where he is weeping and wishing he was back on earth. They ask why he wishes such thing and he replies:

"I wish to come back to earth and put on my finest clothes. Then take my staff and rush through the streets as I knock on every door. I would like to shout at every household, "If you only knew who you are staying away from!"

The thought of touching to every soul and knocking on every door and shouting, "Have faith in God and save yourselves!" has gone through the minds of all Prophets and saints. Unfortunately, human beings are not aware of the games they are playing, the things they are missing out on and where they will end up. One cannot understand human beings who do not think about using lives which was given to them as a one-off capital to earn their eternal lives.

READING TEXT
How Does One Become a Dedicated Person of the Service?

Zübeyr Gündüzalp, a genuine student of Bediüzzaman wrote a letter to Nazım Gökçek of Gaziantep, who was also a student of the *Risale-i Nur* ("Treatise of Light," Bediüzzaman Said Nursi's 6000-page commentary on the Qur'an) explaining the qualities of a person who has dedicated himself to serving the Qur'an:

- Since you inform us that you are willing to tolerate all difficulties in the name of God, you have given us encouragement and passion, therefore listen carefully.

- Your duty is to pick roses amongst the thorns. Your feet are bare hence prickles will pierce them. Your hands are open thus you will have thorns in them. Yet, this will make you happy.

- You will include Moses-like individuals into your ranks, people who were raised in the palace of the pharaohs. For this you will be beaten up. They will incarcerate you for talking but this will make you glad.

- If they cast you into dark dungeons, you will give light; if you come across rusted souls, you will give hope; if you see faithless hearts, you will give Divine light to them. Your giving will be considered as unlawful, you will be will be punished for your thoughts and your speech will send you to prison, yet you will thank the Lord for this.

- You will be separated from your mother, family and loved ones. Yet you will hold firmly onto the Qur'an with your heart. From a drop of water you will become an ocean and from a breath of air you will become a cyclone.

- If you are caught in a storm of lies, smear campaigns and slander, you will not respond with emotions. If they build a barrier of steel in front of you, then you will chew through it with your teeth. If you need to go through a mountain, you will dig into it with a needle.

There is no Greater Duty than Serving Religion

On earth there is no greater duty than serving the religion of God. For if there was such a duty then God would have bestowed it upon His Prophets. The mission of invitation and guidance is the greatest honor given to Prophets and a duty most valued by the side of God. It is rising like the sun to convey the message of God to people so that they could purify themselves and return to their quintessence. Since the time of Prophet Adam, every human being who have accepted this invitation and owned up to this responsibility can in a sense be regarded as those who have sat on the same table with Prophets.

For this reason, a believer should serve his religion with a sense of responsibility and accountability. In regard to this issue, let us take a look at the following story that took place during the time of the late Ottomans. One day, Hüsrev Efendi, one of the latter Ottoman scholars, was explaining a topic to his students. His students noticed a sense of disinclination in the scholar's attitude. They asked: "Teacher, you seem a bit quite and tentative today."

Hüsrev Efendi replied: "Forgive me, I did not wish to make it obvious, but today just before I left home, my daughter passed away. As I was thinking about the funeral arrangements, I remembered that I had a class today. Then I said to myself, "What would God say to me if I neglect my students? Unfortunately, my daughter's body is lying there at home. My mind keeps on going back and forth."

These are the teachers who represent the caravan of eternity and if life is shaped at the hands of such scholars, humanity will reunite with the gratification they are in need of so much.

Let us also provide an example from our time: One day, the principal of a private school operating in a foreign nation sees a child fall down from an open window. The young student had fallen from one of the higher levels of the school building. In panic, the principal rushes out of his office and runs down the stairs. As he runs towards the child, he keeps on thinking, "What would I say to his family? What if this incident affects our service and these people take their students away from us? My God! This incident will certainly bring harm to our educational services!"

As the principal approached the child who was lying on the ground, he uttered the words, "Thank God; it was my child. No harm will come to our service."[12]

It is obvious that there is no difference between Hüsrev Efendi and this young heroic school principal. People who have captured the same horizon of virtue are uniting on the same line. This is an indication of our rediscovery of the sun we had once lost.

Are We Performing Our Duty?

Our noble Prophet was aware of his responsibility. He possessed an unshakable will power and his nerves were made up of steel. He had experienced all forms of difficulties in Mecca yet they did not discourage him a bit. His wife and uncle had passed away one after the other yet he did not lose hope even though they were his greatest supporters in life.

He was given the assignment of being a guide for humanity. He was to explain God to his people, one by one. This was a difficult task yet the Messenger of God had undertaken this without any hesitation. As a result, he made his way into the hearts of human beings.

Even when he was a child, he would repeat the words, "My people... my people!" It was as if he had programmed himself for the assignment that lied ahead. His concerned appearance on the Day of Judgment, standing in two-folds, is the extension of this noble responsibility. In any case, who could possess the endurance to take on such a responsibility but him? It was as if he had taken on the responsibility of all humanity from the first human being to the last.

He lived his live in the same manner, with sensitivity and discipline, from the day he commenced his duty until the day he passed away. The attitude he had when they were a small group made up of one man, one woman, one child and a slave, was the very same attitude when he addressed a crowd of one hundred thousand followers during the farewell Hajj.

---

[12] Akar, Mehmet, *Mesel Ufku*, İstanbul: Timaş, 2008, p. 49

As he delivered his farewell sermon, Muslims gathered to listen to him. His sanctified voice was traveling in radiant spiral waves, reaching all ears and it will continue to echo until the Day of Judgment. For those who were not present, he would say, "Those of you here, convey this to those who are not." The noble Prophet was preparing to leave hence he was uttering his last words:

"O people! I have come to you with a mission. I have explained certain things to you. Tomorrow, on the majestic presence they will ask you if I had accomplished my mission or not. How will you testify to this?"

Indeed, he was a Prophet who had accomplished his mission. He was such a sanctified person that for God, even the distribution of the lock of hair on the side of his face was an important incident in comparison to events which took place in the universe. The Messenger of God was different. He was forgiven for everything that occurred in the pass and everything that would happen in the future. However, he still had concerns. Although, he had completed his mission with success, would his people agree to testify to this? Suddenly, Mount Arafat and Muzdalifa began to tremble with screams. These screams were coming from the deepest corners of the hearts:

"You have fulfilled your mission! You have guided us as a noble Prophet! You are leaving us as a person who has completed his duty!" Upon hearing this, the noble Prophet raised his index finger towards the heavens and shouted: "Be my witness O Lord! Be my witness O Lord! Be my witness O Lord!"[13]

What did the noble Prophet mean by this? Depending on their status and rank, everyone has certain responsibilities and duties. The noble one had completed his duty with great success. How about us? Are we performing our duties in this day and age? This is a question that each and all of us should be asking to ourselves. We cannot become a bystander in front of this blazing fire. We should all be grabbing a bucket and rushing to put it out.

---

[13] *Sunan ibn Majah*, Manasik, 84; *Sunan Abu Dawud*, Manasik, 57

Hiding behind Various Excuses

As we try to perform this Divine duty, we should not be hiding behind various excuses. The following analogy is a good illustration of this:

Once upon time, a war broke out between the land animals and birds. Both sides were struggling to prevail over the other. Bats, which carried the characteristics of both sides, were impartial. When birds ask the bats to join them they would reply: "We are mammals" and when mammals made the same offer; they claimed that they were birds.

Sometime later, the two parties signed a treaty. The bats quickly sided with the birds and congratulated them. However, birds did not accept them into their society. When they tried to join the mammals, they received a similar reception. So the bats were accused of betrayal by both sides. They had no alternatives but to isolate themselves to become prisoners of the dark.

A believer should not come up with excuses to abstain from service. He should light up a candle in the dark and make an effort to support good so that it may prevail over evil. Of course, this should not be done by retribution to evil with evil; on the contrary, it should be done through the representation of good and explaining its beauty.

A soul devoted itself to serving the truth has already accepted the possibility of enduring various difficulties, problems and hardship. A person with such a soul should make an extraordinary effort to fulfill the duty bestowed upon him, in spite of all the difficulties and problems that may arise. He should focus on his objectives and ignore the thousands of problems and burdens he may face. Moreover, as he performs his duty he should take extreme care to stay clear of hiding behind excuses.

This world is a place of worship and service. Life is an episode of time during which the fruits of eternity are planted. Service (Hizmet) can be defined as spreading the Exalted Name of God to the entire humanity hence this mission will always face difficulties as it has many times in the past. Our part in this Divine service is to work relentlessly, without showing reluctance and exhaustion.

Bediüzzaman Has Lived Every Moment of His Troublesome and Difficult Life in the Service of the Qur'an and Faith

In regard to serving faith, Bediüzzaman is one of the foremost role model who should be taken as an example. According to Bediüzzaman, for a believer, serving faith should be the most important objective and goal in life. He has defended this ideal throughout his life and never deviated from such line of thinking. At Eskişehir courthouse, the judge questioned everyone about their occupation and when it was Bediüzzaman's turn, he stood up and said, "My occupation is to serve faith."

Bediüzzaman is a grand pillar who had sacrificed his honor, pride, soul, body and life for the service of the Qur'an and faith. Although he faced all kinds of harassments, insults, tyranny and torture, he did not take a step back from his sanctified duty.

Bediüzzaman sacrificed his worldly comfort to serve religion, abstaining from collecting wealth as he lived in the orbit of contentment, fear of God and piety. Bediüzzaman, a benevolent scholar of Islam and a man of service, spent every minute of his radiant but troublesome life serving the Qur'an. His heart would burn upon seeing the destruction of people at the hands of disbelief and indecency. He would always be involved in invitation to religious activities in the name of "saving faith", saving the people of Muhammad, peace and blessings be upon him, and bringing contentment to humanity. At a time when most people sought after their own personal interests and high status, he dedicated his soul to saving the faith of his people and considered this duty as the greatest mission on earth. The books he had written under most difficult conditions were published for this noble cause. Through the *Risale-i Nur*, he commenced a major scientific campaign against materialism, and enemies of religion and creed. He customized the authentication of notions such as unity, resurrection, Prophethood, justice, destiny, and analytical faith which were being subjected to deformation.

Bediüzzaman was a dedicated man of action and a man, who suffered with the problems of the world of Islam and humanity. He is a hero of service who had devoted his life to the values he sincerely believed. He has never refrained from speaking out what he believed to be the truth. He had been poisoned many times, almost executed on a few occasions and subjected to all kinds of harassments in prison, such as being sent to solitary confinement in freezing conditions when he was an old man, yet he did not make the smallest concession from his beliefs.

Pain and suffering, the two evident signs which have been the companion of those who served on the path of religion were also part of this brilliant man's life.

Bediüzzaman stated, "In my 80 years of life, I do not remember experiencing a moment of worldly pleasure. My life has passed on battle fields, in dungeons, legal courts and prisons. In military courts, I was treated like a murderer and I was sent to exile like a vagrant." These words are a perfect summary of his troublesome life.

Sometimes he would describe the relentless problems that pressurized his soul, with the words, "There were times when I was sick of living. If my religion had permitted suicide, Said would have been dead now." With these words, Bediüzzaman proves that he protected his honor by showing patience and endurance to all forms of tortures he had faced. He kept his entire world packed in a straw basket that he would always carry under his arm. In his view, this is how much the entire world was worth. During the 28 years of life spent in prisons and exile, he taught his students to protect and uphold the law. He never bowed to the oppressive laws of the government but he did not fight against them with force, on the contrary, he used his pen to criticize them. His intelligent and insistent attitude towards "positive behavior" has earned him a unique place in history.

During his sermons, Bediüzzaman would always emphasize on issues like sincerity, brotherhood, faith and the importance of serving the Qur'an, whilst he would frequently caution his students about conceit and egocentric behavior. When Zübeyr Gündüzalp said, "Master, I am afraid of conceit", Bediüzzaman replied, "Be terrified of it." In relation to this, he would give the following advice to his students: "My brothers, our duty is to serve the Qur'an and faith with sincerity. However, our success, people's acceptance and our victory over the oppressors is the duty of God. We will not interfere in this. Even if we are defeated, we will not lose our spiritual willpower and enthusiasm in the service of God. In this sense, we need to be acceptant. Once they said to Jalaladdin Kharzamshah, the great commander of Islam: "You will again be victorious in the battle against Genghis." He replied, "My duty is to strive in God's cause. Victory belongs to the Almighty God. I perform my duty and do not interfere in His."

Bediüzzaman was determined to face all types of difficulties and hardship in the name of serving the Qur'an, sincerity and brotherhood. This attitude had given Bediüzzaman an incredible power of patience. The things they had done to him were outrageous: Summoning him to the police station in the middle of the night, taking him to court at night and interrogating him about his visitors were common harassments for him. If a simple villager kissed his hand, he would be investigated. People who visited him were being harassed constantly. They would say, "Why do you greet him?" "Why do you look at him?" Innocent people were being hassled just for interacting with him. Considering the circumstances, this man of ideals showed great patience in the name of brotherhood as he protected his sincerity.

One of the most important issues that Bediüzzaman focused on was placing values of the Hereafter before everything in life and serving religion without any expectations. Abandoning the service of faith and religion or even showing lethargy towards these imperatives was unacceptable to him.

READING TEXT
"I Have No Fear of Hell Nor Do I Have a Passion for Paradise!"

Bediüzzaman explains his deep inner feelings and thoughts in regard to serving religion to Eşref Edip: "The only thing that gives me anguish is the dangers that Islam faces. In the past, dangers would arrive from an external source. These days, they come from within. The worm has entered the body! It is difficult to resist. I fear that the structure of our society cannot endure this, because it does not detect or recognize the enemy. It assumes its biggest enemy as a friend. This is the enemy that is slashing its main artery and drinking its blood.

If the foresight of society becomes blind, the fortress of faith is in danger. This is my only concern and worry. I do not even have the time to think about the tortures and harassments to which I have been subjected. How I wish that the future of the fortress of faith was sound and safe, then I would not have minded suffering a thousand times more than this!

I am talking sensitively about the structure of our society, its spiritual values, conscience and faith. I teach these things under the light of unity and faith as explained by the Qur'an, because these are the main pillar of society. Society will cease to exist on the day they are shattered.

They asked me, 'Why do you pick on this and that.' I am not even aware of this. There is a blazing inferno in front of me. Its flames are rising to the sky. My children and my faith are smoldering within this fire of disbelief. I am running towards this fire with an aim to extinguish it and save my faith. What logic is there in occupying my-self with someone who wishes to trip me? In the presence of this great danger, what significance does a small incident have?

Do they think that I am a selfish man who thinks about saving himself? I have sacrificed both my world and the Hereafter on the path to saving my society. I have no fear of hell in my heart nor do I have a passion for paradise. For the salvation of twenty five million Turks, let not one Said but a thousand Saids be sacrificed. If our Qur'an is left without followers on earth, I do not want the paradise either. It would become a dungeon for me. I am willing to burn in the flames of hell, if I could only see the salvation of my people. My heart would transform into a rose garden as my body smolders in fire.

In my life of eighty odd years, I do not know of any worldly pleasure. My entire life passed in dungeons, courtrooms and in exile. Indeed, my life has passed with sorrow, agony and hardship. I have sacrificed my world and my own being for the salvation of my society. So let it be! I do not even condemn them. The reason for this is that the *Risale-i Nur* has saved the faith of a few hundred thousand people, this is what they say. According to the prosecutor of Afyon, the Nurs have saved the faith of 500.000 people, perhaps more."

Bediüzzaman was a man prepared to sacrifice his own soul for the salvation of his people. In regards to self-sacrifice, he journeyed on the highest peaks. He forgave those who had tortured and tyrannized him. What kind of a great soul was this?

He would forget all the pain and suffering with one person's acceptance of the sacred truths of faith. He was traveling on the luminous horizon of the Prophets. Who could be more powerful than a person who has total trust and submission in God? How could courts, prisons or death harm him?

"Since the truths of the *Risale-i Nur* are having an effect in the hearts that need faith, let one thousand Saids be sacrificed! I have forgiven those who have tyrannized and tortured me for 28 years. Yes, I have forgiven the people who have banished me from one town to another, people who have insulted and accused me of many things so that they could send me to prison! I have also forgiven those who have cast me into dungeons.

And I say to destiny which is always just, I deserved this slap of compassion. If I had lived like others, thinking about myself only and took the easier path without making any sacrifices from my physical and spiritual emotions, I would have lost this spiritual power to serve faith. I have sacrificed everything I had, both material and spiritual, I have endured all kinds of suffering and I have shown patience to all types of torture. In turn, the reality of faith has spread everywhere. The school of the *Risale-i Nur* has raised thousands, perhaps millions of students. From now on, they will continue on this path of serving faith and they will not deviate from this mission of self-sacrifice. They will work only for the sake of God and only to please Him."[14]

---

[14] Nursi, Bediüzzaman Said. *Risale-i Nur Külliyatı-2*. İstanbul: Nesil, 1996, p. 2206

The Altruistic Heroes of the *Risale-i Nur*

Bediüzzaman, who had spent his life under the shade of the Qur'an and Sunnah was not only a man of deep passion and excitement but also a man of reason and ideals. In his masterpieces, he presents the extensiveness of belief, morals and conscience of the world of Islam in its purest and most effective form. With his profound humanity, fidelity, chastity, humility, sincerity and modesty, he was an extraordinary individual of his era. In contrast to his apparent simplicity, in his thoughts and actions, he was a man of vision and profundity. He was continuously brain storming for the solution of common problems of humanity as he produced solutions under the luminous light of the Qur'an and Sunnah.

Besides being a man of reason and calculation, he was also representing a solid character in his thoughts and actions. He embraced the entire humanity with his thoughts and took a sharp stance against disbelief, tyranny and deviance. Those who were fortunate enough to be around him had witnessed his spiritual depth, prosperous wisdom, high ideals, profundity, simplicity, fidelity and humility. These fortunate souls were the students of the *Risale-i Nur*.

One of the most apparent characteristics of these "firsts" who had gathered around Bediüzzaman was their deep sensitivity towards serving the Qur'an and faith and expecting nothing in return. These people who never made the following claim, "I have served" were extremely effective and beneficial in their efforts as they refrained from materialistic gains, pretension and self-satisfaction. With the permission of God, they were successful in the fields they had served. In facing difficulties and hardship, they would defeat their opponents using their spiritual power of sincerity.

The first heroes of the *Risale-i Nur*, who had taken their master as a role model, had adopted the path of positive action to preserve order in society. Using the *Risale-i Nur*, it was their objective to serve the Qur'an and faith for the sake of God without bringing harm to anyone. They saw no value in themselves. This was the way to serve God; a person had to serve faith purely for the sake of God and in the perception of performing a pure worship. One had to be extra careful in protecting his sincerity, for this reason, one had to refrain from worldly objectives, ranks, positions, fame and fortune. The seeds of service that have engulfed the world like a halo of light in this day and age, was sown by a handful of people who saw no value in this temporary world. They were the people of heart, with no titles and worldly ranks. Their sincerity, altruism, self-sacrifice and distribution of their wealth and health have resulted in the flourishing of today's beautiful service.

Today's Hijra-oriented migration waves to the four corners of the world is nourished by this centralized power. Without doubt, behind this power stands Bediüzzaman who refused to accept even a gift at the size of a grain, along with his unique students such as Hulusi Yahyagil, Hüsrev Altınbaşak, Hafız Ali, Tahiri Mutlu, Zübeyir Gündüzalp, Ceylan Çalışkan, Mustafa Sungur, Bayram Yüksel, Hüsnü Bayram and Abdullah Yeğin.

As Osman Yüksel Serdengeçti explains, Bediüzzaman, who was surrounded by people whose ages ranged from eight to eighty, possessed a profound wisdom in serving the Qur'an and Islam. The people who circled him possessed qualities that could not be described. Contrary to all obstructions, hearts feeling the thirst for faith were constantly running to him. These people of serenity who served the *Risale Nur* were actually walking in the footsteps of those who lived in the Age of Happiness.

With pure and exalted emotions and with the conviction of being connected to an eternal truth, the sincere and loyal sons of Anatolia had gathered around the hero of service, a fortunate man who lived through the Constitutional Era, the period of the Committee of Union and Progress and the Republic to come down from the plateaus of the east with an unshakable faith that kept him upright whilst many disappeared into the pages of history. These fortunate individuals always stood by the side of their master, as he was imprisoned and dragged through execution stools. Alongside Bediüzzaman, they had suffered all forms of harassments, yet using the power originated from their faith, they stood steadfastly and resisted with valor and continued to serve religion throughout their lives.[15]

READING TEXT

The Responsibility Is Big and the Load Is Heavy

The hunters had wounded a bird and the poor animal was trying to escape. It was desperately attempting to fly away but the hunters were chasing it. There was nowhere to hide. Wherever it had hidden, they found it and wherever it landed, they spotted it.

The little bird's heart was pounding with fear. Whenever it stopped for a breather, gun barrels would turn towards it. Hunters were enjoying the challenge; the chase had added an additional excitement to their hunting trip. Compassion had deserted their hearts. They did not even care about the helpless, weak and vulnerable condition of the little bird. They were not going to show any mercy hence would not stop until they killed it. There was a smell of death in the air as gun pallets fired one after another distributing an odor of gun powder to the environment.

The bird had no energy to fly anymore as it made one last desperate attempt to get away. Suddenly, it saw a group of people sitting at a distance. There was a sheikh sitting in middle of the group as they all recited the names of God. The bird used the last of its energy and flew towards the group. With a sudden instinctive action, the little bird flew into the turban of the sheikh to hide. It had found itself a refuge.

The sheikh sensed something moving on his head and with panic he grabbed it. The little bird was in terrible condition hence when the sheikh grabbed it, the poor animal died.

On the Day of Judgment the little bird filed a complaint against the sheikh. The sheikh had not killed the bird intentionally because he did not even know what he had grabbed. Moreover, he felt terrible afterwards when he realized that he had killed a little bird. For this

---

[15] Duman, Murat, *Bir Fikir ve Aksiyon İnsanı Bediüzzaman Said Nursi*. İstanbul: Gelecek, 2008

reason, he was not held accountable. They asked the bird for a last statement and it said:

"I have a request. I took refuge under that turban with trust thinking that I would be protected. From now on, people who fail to honor this trust should not be permitted to wear the turban so that others do not fall into same situation as I did."

The moral of the story is that our generation is looking for a shelter so that they can protect themselves from the merciless traps of the hunters. Humanity has fallen into the swamp of sins. Humanity is struggling and weeping as it sinks deeper and deeper into the quicksand. Humanity is responsible of every teenager that has become a heroin addict because no one has reached out to them and it is liable for every teenager who has lost their chastity, no matter which nationality, race or color they are. Hospitals, prisons and cemeteries are crying out for help!

This is a big responsibility and our load is heavy. No one has the right to break the trust of those who are fleeing from this fire and reaching out for help. Since we cannot remove the garment of faith from our shoulders, then we should show great effort to honor the turban.[16]

One Should Not Have Expectation on the Path of Service

A believer should not have materialistic or spiritual expectations when serving the religion. In one of his conversations, Fethullah Gülen describes this notion with the following words:

"Our part is to serve without any expectations. Whether it is here or somewhere else, one should serve without any worldly expectations. I always say to my fellow students, 'Spread around the world. Do not expect a paycheck or scholarship. Be a laborer, dish washer or cleaner and earn your living but serve your people and religion.' If you have the talent then write something, publish a book. If you have no other

---

[16]   Akar, Mehmet, *Mesel Ufku*, İstanbul: Timaş, 2008, p. 103

option, then become a garbage collector but never expect something in return. Otherwise, you will miss these days in the future."[17]

When it comes to serving, a believer should take the front row but when it comes to wages, he should stand at the very back hence he should not have any expectations. A person of service should expect his rewards only from the Almighty God. He should not have expectations from anyone else. People of service, who have no other wish than to please God, should be aware of the fact that this transient world is not a place of rewards. They should be in the comprehension of "rewards for their services will be given on the Hereafter"; hence they should be working relentlessly without having the slightest of expectation.

For example, one of the most important things is to raise a good generation. The best investment is the one that is made on a human being, in particular the youth. The youth of today will serve their nation and humanity in the future as adults.

One day, the Companions had gathered in a meeting. Umar ibn Khattab was asking them one by one: "You wish to serve Islam. If God was to accept your prayer, what would you ask of him in the name of serving Islam?"

One of them replied: "If my prayer was to be accepted, I would ask for a chest of gold. I would use all of it to serve Islam."

Umar put the same question to another person sitting beside him, he replied: "I would also ask for a chest full of treasure and I would use all the silver coins to serve Islam."

Another person said: "I would ask from God a herd of sheep so big that it would fill the desert. I would distribute the milk and the meat of these animals to Muslims and serve Islam this way."

Finally, the Companions asked Umar what he would pray for. Umar replied: "If God was to give me whatever I wish, I would not ask for silver, gold, sheep or camels. I would ask for loyal men. Men like Abu Ubayda, Abu Dharr and Muaz ibn Jabal."

Indeed, raising a blessed generation is the most important thing.

[17] Ünal, İsmail, *Fethullah Gülen'le Amerika'da Bir Ay*, İstanbul. Nil, 2001, p. 78

READING TEXT

Where Have You Been All This Time?

A man of service explains: It was the year 1994. I was late for a lecture to which I was going to attend with my friends. I expressed my apologies and explained that I visited a friend who had lost someone. It was an interesting incident which resulted with death. Just prior to his death the man had received four phone calls from his son, daughter and son-in-laws.

He was surprised by the phone calls that came one after another, although he replied "I am well" to all of them, he thought to himself, "There is something strange here." A few minutes later he had died sitting in his sofa. The entire incident had occurred within half an hour. When I explained this to the people at the gathering, a young man said, "Allow me to explain a similar incident" and continued: Your warm friendship and these conversations have affected me a lot. We have only met recently yet I always think to myself, "Why couldn't I find these people before." As you can see I only have one arm. Let me tell you about my accident and the events preceding it. My fiancé İpek and I were getting married in ten days time. On that particular day I picked her up from her house and then we went to a bar. Later, a friend of mine and another friend whose name was also Murat came to the bar with their girlfriends. I was not expecting them, so I said, "What are you guys doing here?" They began to laugh and shouted, "We came to die!" We replied, "We came for the same reason" and laughed along.

A few minutes later another friend named Hakan came in with two girls. Normally, this was a time that we would not be there hence this is why I asked the same question to him, "Why are you doing here?" Unaware of what went on before, he replied, "We came to die!" We had a few drinks and laughed. Later, we walked out of the bar. I gave my car keys to Hakan and we jumped into Murat's car. That night, İpek seemed a bit strange. I wanted to sit in the back and I asked İpek to sit in the middle, between me and the other girl. However, no matter how much I insisted, she asked me to sit in the middle. Murat was driving the car and he had his girlfriend sitting at the front passenger seat.

We drove away from the bar and a short while after we had a terrible accident. Murat, İpek and the girl on my other side had died instantly. I was in a coma. The girl at the front had survived the accident without a scratch. She had opened the door and walked away without even looking back.

When the police arrived at the scene, they thought we were all dead. The ambulance had taken us to the morgue of the nearby hospital. Later, when they came in for identity verification, someone realized that I was still alive. They told me later that I had moved and then screamed when the morgue door was opened. I heard that one of the police officers was deeply affected by the incident that he received psychiatric treatment for a few months.

One of my arms was amputated and my treatment in the country and abroad took several months. Later, I found out that Hakan and his passengers in the other car were also involved in the accident and died. There were only two survivors, the other girl and me.

As Murat was telling his story, we all held our breaths and listened with pure attention. Then he continued: A few months after the accident I found out something incredible. My friend Murat, who shared the same name as me, had prepared a grave for himself, 15 days prior to the accident. He even called a hodja and asked him to recite the Qur'an over the grave. The hodja said, "How can I read the Qur'an to this grave, it is empty." Murat had replied, "You make the prayer, its occupant will come soon."

Following the accident, they had buried Murat in that grave. Interestingly, my fiancé İpek had gathered her dresses and packed them up in a luggage just before I had picked her up that evening. She had also left a note next to the luggage, "If I don't return, give these clothes to poor families or to children's refuge." I knew that she had sensed the accident that night. She loved me so much that she insisted I sit in the middle. She wanted to protect me because I had never seen her to be stubborn like that.

As Murat explained this, he began to weep and then asked: "She believed in God and she did not drink alcohol. She was honest and altruistic. She enjoyed helping people. Because of the way she was raised, she did not know much about religion. Do you think that God will forgive her?"

We tried to console him by explaining that God has infinite mercy hence His mercy will also encompass a person who was raised in an era which resembles the time of *fatrat* (an era when people have no Prophet to guide them). Moreover, one cannot lose hope in the mercy of God.

Murat continued by talking about himself: "I believe in God. I have not touched a drink for the past year. However, I have stayed away from my religion for too long. I did not know these things and no one reached out to me before. Would I be forgiven by God?"

Again we explained about the vastness of God's mercy. His eyes sparkled as he smiled. He said, "I never want to leave you guys, thus with your permission I wish to join all your gatherings." With pure sincerity we answered, "We are expecting you."

The following week, he had gathered all the newspaper clips about the accident and he wanted to bring them to us. However, after the accident he began to have epileptic seizures and that evening he had a seizure and İsmail Bey drove him back to his home. When he recovered he called and said he was sorry because he could not attend the previous lecture. We were told that a week later he had another seizure and fallen in the shower. He hit his head and they took him to the hospital. When we visited him at the hospital, he did not recognize us. A few days after the incident, Murat also passed away.

All the youth who lived in Bağdat Avenue (in İstanbul) were crying for this young man. They were all at the funeral. When they realized who we were, they all came next to us. One of them said, "After meeting you guys, Murat came to us. He said that he had made beautiful new friends. He wanted us to meet you guys also. He said that our path was not a good path. He also explained to us that everything in this world was transient and ephemeral. He wished to live

Islam and encouraged us to participate in your gatherings. He was going to introduce you to us but his life was cut short."

Murat had made the most of the little time God had blessed. After the funeral, we visited his family. His mother and sister also said that Murat loved to be with us.

At the funeral there was also a young man who had bandages on his head. He approached us and said, "Murat was my best friend and I loved him. When I heard about his death, I smashed my car by driving into a wall. This is when I hurt my head. I want to say something to you guys, did Murat had to die so that we could meet each other? Why didn't you reach out to us before?"

Later on, we found out that Murat was an extremely generous young man. Following İpek's death he had become even more benevolent. Currently, he rests in the grave he had prepared next to İpek at the Karacaahmet Cemetery.[18]

God Will Help You If You Support His Religion

In the Qur'an God says, "*O you who believe! Keep from disobedience to God in reverent piety, with all the reverence that is due to Him, and see that you do not die save as Muslims (submitted to Him exclusively)*" (Al Imran 3:102). This verse means you should have a firm footing on the ground; you should protect your heart and never forget why you were created; and it also commands that you should honor the covenant. This is a covenant which was made between our Lord and us. A verse in Surah al-Baqarah confirms this: "... *fulfill My covenant (which I made with you through your Prophets), so that I fulfill your covenant, and of Me alone be in awe and fear (in awareness of My Power and of your being My servants)*" (al-Baqarah 2:40).

The pledge made here is to acknowledge Him, explain Him to others and to worship Him accordingly. If this is fulfilled, then He will show mercy on His servants and bless them with the eternal paradise.

Having both feet firmly on the ground has another meaning and it is illuminated with the following verse from the Qur'an: "*O you who*

---

[18] Refik, İbrahim, *Hadiselerin İbret Dili*, İstanbul: Albatros, 2000, p. 98

believe! If you help God (by striving in His cause), He will help you and make your feet firm (so that you are steadfast in His cause and ultimately victorious)" (Muhammad 47:7). No one can provide aid to God and God does not need the aid of anyone. What the verse actually means is to support the religion of God and to make an effort to spread His exalted Name. Those who support the religion of the All-Merciful here will be supported by the All-Merciful in the life after. God will grant them the blessing of entering the grave with faith and He will keep their feet firmly on the ground throughout their lives.

This is valid for both parties, those who guide others and those who are being guided. In the Hereafter, many wonderful surprises await these people. A young man named Safa, who studies in Central Asia, explains: "There was friend who was studying on a government scholarship. We were in the same faculty studying in the same class. He had graduated from a technical college. He was staying at an accommodation provided by the university. During the summer holidays he went home and his father sensed a change in him and said, "Son, it seems like everything is lawful to you, I will not send you back there." He insisted that his father permit him to go back arguing that his education was important to him. His father replied, "I will let you go on one condition. If you stay with good mannered, virtuous friends, I will consider it." He accepted his father's condition.

It was the beginning of a new semester; he came to me and explained the situation. He asked if he could stay with us. He said, "This is my father's condition, in order to continue my education I have to stay with you guys." I said to him, "It can be arranged but I have to speak with the others." Quickly, I spoke to my friends and explained the situation. They said that he did not have a good reputation and this could also affect us. No matter how much I insisted, I could not get them to accept.

Every day he would pull me aside and ask, "What happened? Did you speak to them?" I kept on making excuses by saying, "I will speak to them soon." I thought that eventually he would give up. However, he never gave up. So, I continued to apply pressure on my roommates. One they my roommates said, "If you are so keen on this then why don't you go and live with him." I said ok then I will do that. I took a few other friends along and rented a place. Then I invited him to live with us. Before long, his attitude and behavior began to change. He abandoned some of his bad habits and developed himself. Sometime later, he became a new person where even his face and heart began to glow. All the neighbors and friends who visited us loved him. One day he became severely ill. We took him to the hospital. The doctor said, "You are too late, his appendix has burst." For some reason, he had not noticed it. The leak had also caused serious damage to other organs. There was no hope for him hence the doctor advised us to call his relatives so that they could see him one last time. His father came quickly and caught him taking his last breath.

A few months later I saw him in a dream. He was sitting on the ground drinking tea whilst we conversed. He was sitting on one side of me and I had another friend sitting on the other side. I asked him, "How did they treat you there?" He replied, "I was treated as one of you. Here they do not cast people like you into hellfire. This is why I was also blessed with paradise." When I woke up, I wept loudly for a long time. The effects of that dream did not wear off for many hours." [19]

The glad tiding conveyed by Bediüzzaman is, in this day and age those who serve faith and the Qur'an will be saved by the will of God. He adds that the people of service are "The people of faith and salvation."

God has the power to transform the little effort made by those who choose His path into a lot. He is the All-Munificent. The doors of mercy will be opened wide to anyone who knocks on it with sincerity. For as long as, we do not deviate from the radiant path, the eternal caravan, justice and truth.

READING TEXT

The Souls We Have Been Looking Forward To

We have heard a lot, seen a lot, and rolled through many different events, but we failed to shake off sorrow and find peace. We failed to

---

[19] Akar, Mehmet, *Mesel Ufku*, İstanbul: Timaş, 2008, p. 138

be contented in our feelings and find inner peace; since our needs and the cures offered were completely different.

We were expecting apostles to extend a hand to the transgressor and sinner, to cry along with broken hearts—apostles with touching words, lively spirits, and serious speech.

For years, we have been waiting for men of truth who offer consolations we securely receive, to whom we can open up the depths of our heart sincerely, whose faith and sagacity is as sound as mountains. As famine, disease, and fear befell us successively, as the most shameful miseries ate away our souls and eroded our wills, we always felt beside us their reviving breath vitalizing us with hope.

If only we could find what we have felt and sensed so far and if only we believed in what we found, so many gaps would have been filled, so many obstacles would have been overcome. However, perhaps a thousand times we got together, filled with hopes, made up our mind for a start, and perhaps a thousand times broke our oath; since we could not find what we sought, and we could not see what we sought in what we found.

We had hearts thirsty for compassion and love, asking for benevolence and humanity. Alas! Our spirits were led to misery and they tried to immerse our hearts in every kind of crudeness. We were receiving a raw deal, and eating our hearts out in never-ending fits. In our terrible condition under every kind of oppression, disgrace, and misery, we were constantly abused and victimized by greedy passions.

This is why now we cannot believe anybody and cannot attach our hearts to anyone. "When we want a beautiful woman picking up roses, we also want that she has red cheeks; when we want the conqueror of Khaybar [Ali ibn Abu Talib], we also want his loyal servant Kambar." (Muhammed Lutfi). We may find it or not, but having been overwhelmed by trouble we want now purity, sincerity, and dedication in the path of these "blind lovers."

After having seen so much neglect, even betrayal, overcoming our doubts and approaching the people we meet with tolerance seems like naivety to us. In spite of all our good intentions and tolerant attitude, we cannot overcome our doubts and break through the atmosphere of lack of trust.

Making us believe and removing our doubts depends on the continuity of sincere acts of our heroes. Thanks to these sincere and convincing acts, we will be able to shake off the ill opinion and lack of trust we have been carrying on our backs for years.

We are fed up with lip-service invitations, brazen manners, and false heroism after already-won victories, fervent desires to enjoy worldly life, greed for fortune, and seeking worldly rank. What we expect from our Hercules is a sound will to bring water from beyond the furthest mountains, convincing determination in his actions, building his victories through personal endeavor, sacrificing material or spiritual benefits with a desire to make others live, holding no expectancies, and altruism.

Let their thoughts be pure and untainted, let the roads be straight and free of zigzags. Let them think, live, and tell what they lived. Let them never be hypocritical and not deceive us.

Let there be the lines of grief and suffering on their faces. Let their eyes be wet with tears, their bosoms be deep, and consciences alive. Let them adopt the self-criticism and nobility of the Sufi path, the logic and reasoning of the schools, and the discipline and obedience of the military; let them attain perfection through these.

Let them help our people—whose hearts and minds have been detached, whose soul is deprived of the conscience, and who is invited to only corporeality—be saved from their depression of centuries, and may they be returned to their own nature.

Let them hold the truth dear, not take their own thoughts and way of servitude as the only righteous path, and not forget for a moment that the ways leading to God are as many as the breaths of creation.

Let them be eager to serve and be in the first ranks, but to stay behind when it comes to receiving wages and benefits. And at least, like Cato the Elder (who gained victories, but preferred to be a humble farmer after the campaigns), they should stand aside after having fulfilled their responsibility toward their people and humbly wait until another duty is given.

The pioneers of this blessed path avoided seeking worldly rank. When they had to assume authority, they sincerely and insistently wished for others with the required potential to take charge.

Those who volunteer for a new project of revival have to keep up in this line. Otherwise, the fuss raised by the imbalance between limited positions and numerous greedy eyes will be unavoidable and difficult. Especially, if this notion is reflected on the immature and energized souls of the young people!

I wonder whether we can ever see utter sincerity from these people whom we have been expecting as apostles. Anyway, we will once more emphasize our desperate need of these souls like air and water and implore God Almighty with the tongue of everything—the fish in the sea and the gazelle in the mountains—and beseech Him not to make us wait so long.[20]

Do We Need the Permission of Our Parents to Serve Our Religion?

The most obvious example in this regard is Ali. It was during the early days of Prophethood. The noble Prophet was observing the Prayer with Khadija, may God be pleased with her. Ali was only ten as he watched them with great admiration. At the conclusion of the Prayer, he asked, "What were you doing?"

The Messenger of God replied, "O Ali, this is a religion that God chose and He is pleased with. I am inviting you to believe in the One and only God. I am averting you from worshipping the idols that can do no benefit nor harm to human beings."

Ali paused for a moment and then replied, "This is something that I had never heard before. I have to ask my father first." That day Ali did not tell anyone about the conversation he had with the Messenger of God. He thought about the whole thing throughout the night. A light emerged in his heart at dawn. Quickly he went to the

[20] Gülen, M. Fethullah, *Çağ ve Nesil*, İstanbul: Nil, 2011, pp. 18–21

noble Messenger of God and said, "When God created me, He did not ask for my father's permission. So, why should I ask for the permission of Abu Talib, in regards to believing God and worshiping Him?"[21] This gave Ali the honor of being the first Muslim child.

Indeed, Ali was to believe in the God Who created him and therefore worship Him. Asking for his father's advice and opinion on this issue did not make any sense.

For this reason, it is the primary duty of a believer to serve his religion. However, in doing so, one must not break the heart of his parents and behave in an offensive manner.

The only time that a believer can refuse to obey his parents is if they say, "Do not serve your faith and religion!" the Holy Qur'an states:

> But if they strive with you to make you associate with Me something of which you certainly have no knowledge (and which is absolutely contrary to Knowledge), do not obey them. Even then, treat them with kindness and due consideration in respect of (the life of) this world. Follow the way of him who has turned to Me with utmost sincerity and committed himself to seeking My approval. Then (O all human beings), to Me is your return, and then I will make you understand all that you were doing (and call you to account). (Luqman 31:15)

Indeed, parents should always be respected and appreciated. However, they should not be obeyed in situations of rebellion against God. A person who obeys his parents when they should be obeyed will have a prosperous, affluent earnings and knowledge. Sooner or later, God will honor such people and many past experiences can be provided as solid evidence to this reality.

Believers who serve on the path of God should be in awareness of the enormity and significance of their service. Let us beseech from the mercy of the Almighty that He increases the enthusiasm of our brothers and honors us with the opportunity to serve His religion. Conversely, on this path, those who have attained a certain level through zeal and love can lose this Divine favor if they slow

---

[21] Ibn Hisham, *As-Sirah*, 1/264

down the tempo or fail to preserve their enthusiasm, passion, excitement and sincerity in service. In order to avoid this, they should at least protect what they already have, so that it is not taken away from them to be given to someone else. This is the custom of the Creator. For this reason, besides making an effort on His path, one should also knock on the doors of His mercy continuously through prayers so that he is not refused or pushed out. May God allow us to serve His religion and may He protect our vitality.

QUESTIONS

1. He was the son of a wealthy Meccan family. He was a kind, handsome and civilized young man. He chose a virtuous life and turned his back to his family's wealth. Following the first Aqaba Pledge, our noble Prophet sent him to Medina with the new Muslims, so that he could teach Islam and recite the Qur'an to them. Who was this Companion of the Prophet?
   a. Mus'ab ibn Umayr
   b. Asad ibn Zurara
   c. Bilal
   d. Umar ibn Khattab

2. *"God burdens no soul except within its capacity: in its favor is whatever (good) it earns, and against it whatever (evil) it merits"* (al-Baqarah 2:286).
   Which of the below statements concur with the verse above?
   a. God will load people with duties they cannot carry, such as the Hajj.
   b. Human beings have the power to do anything.
   c. There is no "a burden greater than a soul can bear" (people will not be held responsible for duties they cannot bear or carry).
   d. God forces His servants into performing worship.

3. Who was the Companion invited to Islam at the age of ten. He embraced Islam after making the following statement "God did not ask my father before He created me, so why should I

ask my father, Abu Talib for permission to believe in God
and worship?"
a. Abu Bakr
b. Umar
c. Uthman
d. Ali

4. What is the meaning of the following prayer: "*Allahummar-
    ham ummata Muhammad.*"
    a. "O God make us the members of the *ummah* of Muham-
        mad"
    b. "O God, show mercy to the *ummah* of Muhammad"
    c. "O God, make all human beings a part of Muhammad's
        ummah."
    d. "O God, sanction the *ummah* of Muhammad to love me."

5. "Taking a step on the path to pleasing God with an intention
    to strive in God's cause and for humanity's good is more
    blessed than ...." Fill in the blank
    in the above *hadith* with one of the options provided below:
    a. everything you possess
    b. everything you will possess
    c. everything in the world
    d. the Paradise

6. Who is the scholar who came to class even on the day that his
    beloved daughter had died; arguing that "What would God
    say to me if I neglect my students?"
    a. Hüsrev Efendi
    b. M. Fethullah Gülen
    c. Mehmet Akif Ersoy
    d. Bediüzzaman Said Nursi

7. Which of the word synonyms below is incorrect?
    a. Responsibility – Liability
    b. Gradual – Hastily
    c. Duty – Obligation
    d. Pure – Unpolluted

8. Which statement below is not valid in regard to serving religion and God?

    a. We should learn our religion in the best way possible.

    b. We should be patient, tolerant and kind.

    c. We should explain the virtues of faith patiently and gradually, and we should practice what we preach.

    d. We should serve religion after we finish our studies and attain a career for ourselves.

9. Which of the statements below is correct?

    a. One must obey his/her parents even if they command rebellion against God.

    b. One must always behave benevolently towards his parents, but should not obey them only in situations where they ask one to rebel against God or His commandments.

    c. In order to serve religion one must get the permission of his parents, otherwise he cannot serve religion.

    d. One cannot embrace faith without the permission of his elders and parents.

10. Which commander replied "My duty is to strive in God's cause. Victory belongs to the Almighty God. I perform my duty and do not interfere in His" when they said to him "You will again be victorious in the battle against Genghis"?

    a. Jalaladdin Kharzamshah

    b. Yavuz Sultan Selim

    c. Salahaddin Ayyubi

    d. Fatih Sultan Mehmed

2

STRIVING IN GOD'S CAUSE, INVITATION AND GUIDANCE

Prophet Muhammad, upon him be peace and blessings, called upon us to protect religion, life, reason, property and the integrity of family and lineage, and to strive for this purpose. In a remarkably balanced way, he proclaimed that no other duty could equal this struggle.[22]

S triving in God's cause (*jihad*) has various meanings such as overcoming all forms of difficulties and struggles to make an effort, to exert energy and to work vigorously. In another definition, Striving in God's cause is the effort exerted on removing all barriers between God and His servants. All projects initiated in the name of God, all efforts made so that His Name and religion are glorified and all forms of struggle experienced in the defense of His sacred values can be defined as "striving in God's cause and for humanity's good."

For a believer, spending and utilizing gifts and blessings such as the physical body, intelligence and wealth—which were entrusted upon human beings by God—on the path of God, would also be considered as such a striving.

As the meaning of the word defines, *jihad* is not an offense; rather it is a defense against a possible offence. It is the effort made to block an offence. In a way, it means removing all obstacles from the path that lead to human contentment.

---

[22] Gülen, M. Fethullah, *Pearls of Wisdom*, New Jersey: Tughra Books, 2012, p. 8

According to another definition, it is to serve God as this is the objective of life; learning the principles of religion and implementing them as they are taught by God and His Messenger; commanding the doing of good and working to prevent evil; a struggle done against the carnal desires which always command evil and the enemies of universal virtues; and also protecting a country from all external threats and attacks. In this sense *jihad* caries a comprehensive meaning hence it can be carried out by using the heart, tongue and the hands.

Arguing that *jihad* is all about war does not reflect the entire truth. Moreover, giving this word a definition which is restricted to war would be considered as a deficient interpretation according to the many meanings it carries in the Qur'an and the *hadith*s.

The objective of *jihad* is to take the name of God to humanity; to glorify the banner of faith; to defend people from oppression and tyranny; to remove all obstacles between virtues and human beings and to give people the opportunity of an easy access to high morality. [23]

The decree of *jihad* varies depending on certain conditions and situations. In some situations it is *fard al-ayn* (personal obligations for each and every individual Muslim) and in some situations it is *fard al-kifaya* (community obligations—for the health and welfare of the wider community but in no way binging upon the individual).

If a group amongst Muslims is fulfilling the requirements of *jihad* by protecting the nation, wealth, chastity and honor of Muslims, then it has become a *fard al-kifaya*, hence the responsibility has been removed from the other Muslims.

Jihad as Described in the Qur'an and *Hadith*

The term is mentioned forty times in the Qur'an within different context and framework. Where in some verses *jihad* indicates to war, in others it carries the meaning: an effort made to live in accordance with the approval and acceptance of God.[24]

---

[23] Ünlü, Selman, *Adını Kalplere Yazmak*, İstanbul: Rehber, 2006, pp. 18–20
[24] Al-Baqarah 2:154, 216; Al Imran 3:146, 169; an-Nisa 4:76; at-Tawbah 9:36, 41

Our noble Prophet stated, "Faith and striving in God's cause and for humanity's good on the path of God are the most virtuous of all deeds."[25] However, he also added that, "The real *mujahid* is the individual who performs *jihad* with his own carnal soul."[26]

Abu Hurayra explains: "One of the Companions of the Prophet travelled through a mountainous track where he discovered a waterhole. He fell in love with this place so much that he said, 'I wish I could live here all alone, away from society. However, I cannot do this without the permission of the Prophet.' Later, he explained his wish to the noble Prophet and the Messenger of God said: 'Do not think about this, because, it is more virtuous for one of you to perform *jihad* on the path of God than to stay in his home and pray for seventy years. Would you not want God to forgive you and place you in Paradise? Then perform *jihad* on the path of God. Whoever performs *jihad* on the path of God even for a short period, a time that it takes to milk a camel, he will definitely enter Paradise.'"[27]

There are many *hadith*s in relation to the merits of *jihad* and we will mention some of them later in our topic.[28]

How Many Types of *Jihad* Are There?

When they returned from the Expedition of Tabuk, the noble Messenger of God said to his Companions: "We are returning from the lesser *jihad* to the greater *jihad*." When his Companions asked what could be a greater *jihad* than fighting on the battle field, he replied: "*Jihad* with your carnal soul (*nafs*)."[29] With this statement, he had divided *jihad* into two main parts: the greater *jihad* and the lesser *jihad*.

The greater *jihad* can be described as taming the carnal soul by refraining from what is prohibited by Islam and observing the obliga-

---

[25] *Sahih Muslim*, Imara, 117; *Sunan at-Tirmidhi*, Jihad, 32
[26] *Sunan at-Tirmidhi*, Fadailu'l-Jihad, 2
[27] *Ibid.*, 17
[28] *Sahih Muslim*, Imara, 163; *Sunan at-Tirmidhi*, Fadailu'l-Jihad, 12; *Sunan Abu Dawud*, Jihad 18; *Sunan an-Nasa'i*, Jihad 1; *Sahih Muslim*, Imara, 172; *Sunan ibn Majah*, Fitan, 20
[29] Munawi, *Fayd al-Qadir*, Daru'l-Fikr, 4/511; Ajluni, *Kashf al-Khafa*, Cairo, 1/511

tory acts of worship; living according to the teachings of the elevated Sunnah and abstaining from everything that is considered as evil by Islam; making an effort to convey what is learned about religion and truth to family members, relatives, friends and everyone within range; ignoring the gossip and vilification made by others and continuing on the path of God with consistency and reliability.

Without doubt, the most difficult *jihad* is the one made against the carnal soul and carnal desires. Those who fail to establish victory over their carnal desires will not have the courage or strength to stand before the enemy. The following *hadith* authenticates this reality: "A real *mujahidin* is a person who performs *jihad* against his own carnal soul."[30]

As for the lesser *jihad*, a person who has achieved success in the greater *jihad* will certainly run to the frontlines when faith and its sacred values need to be protected from the enemy.

A struggle given on the path of God occurs at two fronts: inner and outer. The inner struggle can be defined as one's attempt to return to his true quintessence and the outer struggle can be described as one's effort to return others to their quintessence. The main objective in the first is to overcome all barriers set by the carnal soul to find God hence to reach spiritual fulfillment. The main objective in the second front is to remove all barriers which were placed on the path to God so that everyone can get the opportunity to find God and acknowledge Him. The balance is established when *jihad* is performed at both fronts, otherwise the concept of *jihad* would be ruined.

The meaning intended by the greater *jihad* is one's ascend to humanity in his spiritual and metaphysical worlds. Such *jihad* means that one needs to be in constant struggle with his carnal desires, even during basic activities such as eating, drinking or strolling. That is to say, one must fight against all desires that God is not pleased with, throughout his life.

---

[30] *Sunan at-Tirmidhi*, Fadailu'l-Jihad, 2

Whereas, the lesser *jihad* means to struggle on the path of God with one's wealth and life and if required protect the values of faith and religion by engaging in all forms of combat, including war.

According to the definitions above, the greater *jihad* exists at all times throughout one's life under all conditions and situations, but the lesser *jihad* is a duty carried out only when it becomes necessary.

The Noble Prophet Experienced the Greater and the Lesser *Jihad* at the Highest Level

We observe that our noble Prophet had fulfilled the responsibility of the greater and the lesser *jihad* at the highest level. On the battle fields, he was a symbol of heroism and gallantry. A man like Ali who was a model gallantry explains that during the battle when the going got really tough, the Companions would take refuge behind the noble Prophet.

The Messenger of God who was a hero of gallantry also held the highest peak when it came to servanthood and worship. As described in the *hadith*, his Prayers would remind you of a boiling pot; he would touch the hearts of everyone when he wept and shed his noble tears. At times, he would fast for many days. And at times, he would pray throughout the night until his feet were swollen. Once our mother Aisha asked, "O Messenger of God, why are you stressing yourself so much when God has already forgiven your past and future sins?" He replied, "O Aisha, should I not be a grateful servant?"[31]

He was a man of spirituality and of heart during both the physical and metaphysical jihads. He would constantly encourage his people to repent by saying, "Every day, I repent more than seventy times."[32]

Without question, attaining victory in the lesser *jihad* depends on its participants' consistency and success in the greater *jihad* done with the carnal soul. If a person struggling for the truth on every platform does not practice its realities in his own private world, he will never succeed in the lesser *jihad*.

---

[31] *Sahih al-Bukhari*, Tafsir as-Surah (48), 2; *Sahih Muslim*, Munafiqun, 81
[32] *Sahih al-Bukhari*, Dawat, 3

When we scrutinize history with caution, we will see that those who had fulfilled their duties of invitation to the universal virtues with great success have always journeyed through the same path. Indeed, from the Prophets to the great scholars, they all followed the very same path. In return, God had blessed them with a powerful and effective speech complementary to the sincerity they had displayed. Moreover, God has blessed them a great success for the enthusiasm they had shown and sited them in history as symbols of sweet memories that should be taken as role models.

As the noble Messenger of God spread the word of truth without rest and weariness, his Companions did the same by travelling to the four corners of the world and trying to spread virtues at the highest level possible.

As the Companions took this universal religion to the four corners of the world, they were quite aware of their responsibilities. With great zeal and valor they were rushing from one front to another, performing *jihad* and making an effort to display their loyalty to God so that they could behold the Divine Beauty in Paradise.

They were devoted to a Divine cause and for this reason worldly life had no value in their eyes. The passion that others showed for living was manifesting in them as a passion for reunion with God. This zeal for reunion with God was so intense that they were burning up with it. Their infatuation was so obvious that a commander of the Byzantium army once said to his king: "Sire! We cannot fight these men. As much as we fear and flee from death, they ran to it with passion!"

The loyalty of the Companions to the Messenger of God and their moral, physical and financial support to faith is mind boggling. For this reason, God has mentioned them in His Divine Book before all else and revealed that they deserved His blessings by highlighting that He is pleased with them.

The fidelity displayed by Muslim women on this path is also noteworthy. When the noble Messenger was about to embark on his *jihad*, these women would bring all the jewelry they possessed such as necklaces, bracelets and earrings and give them to the noble Messenger of God, willingly and without any hesitation.[33]

About *Jihad*

Jihad is sometimes interpreted as "Holy War." There is a reason for this interpretation and that is to give the impression that Islam is a religion which is spread by the force of the sword. However, the term *jihad* does not exclusively mean war. Whilst, *jihad* also includes the meaning of striving on the path of God, the real definition of the term contains all forms of action and efforts exerted on the path of spreading the universal virtues to the four corners of the world.

Whatever a Muslim does, he/she does it for the sake of God. Islam's perspective of life is clearly described in the following verses in the Qur'an:

> Those who (truly) believe fight in God's cause, while those who disbelieve fight in the cause of *taghut* (powers of evil who institute patterns of rule in defiance of God). So (O believers), fight against the friends and allies of Satan. Assuredly, Satan's guile is ever-feeble. (an-Nisa 4:76)

Muslims have also participated in battles. However, in these battles the concept was not to convert people to Islam by force, but to liberate people who were oppressed and were not given the opportunity to practice and spread their religion. It was to form a medium where everyone could live and practice their religion freely. For this reason, such historical campaigns were given the title of *fath* (conquest); this was done intentionally so that they could be distinguished from invasion and incursion.

What is the Greatest *Jihad*?

The noble Prophet constantly repeated the following prayer: "O God! Do not leave me alone with my carnal soul even for a blink of an eye."[34]

---

[33] Aydüz, Davut, "Tebliğ Hizmetinde Ashabın Fedakarlıkları", *Yeni Ümit*, 66, 2004
[34] Al-Hakim, *Mustadrak*, 1/545

Moreover, he advised Muslims with the following *hadith*: "Return to the greater *jihad* from the lesser *jihad*."[35] These words teach us that no *jihad* is more difficult than the one that is made with the carnal soul.

The greatest *jihad* is the one that is performed against the greatest enemy. "Your biggest and most detrimental enemy is your carnal soul."[36] This *hadith* clearly defines the carnal soul as the biggest enemy. Just as the carnal soul must be defeated before going to a war; it should also be defeated before one begins to invite people to virtues. *Jihad* with the carnal soul is imperative. Every moment of our lives pass with this kind of *jihad*. A slightest negligence could cost us dearly. The physical *jihad* is not continuous. For this reason, during time of peace, Muslims will not be held accountable for this kind of *jihad*.[37]

In order to perform *jihad* under the current conditions, we must produce intellectual Muslim scholars, publish various journals, papers and keep them running, publish books that explain Islam in the most beautiful way, establish libraries and organize conferences, lectures, seminars and conversations. We must volunteer for various aid campaigns and make the most of such campaigns to encourage those around us.

In another *hadith*, our noble Prophet states: "The mission begins with Islam, the Prayer is its pillar and *jihad* is its peak."[38]

Issues That Impede on *Jihad*

There are certain matters that impede on *jihad* just they do on all good deeds. The first impediment is our carnal soul, the second is the Satan and the third is the external enemies. Resisting the carnal temptations of the carnal soul is considered as *jihad*. Walking on the right path and closing one's ears to the whispers of Satan is also regarded as *jihad*. Finally, combating with the enemies of God who try to block-

---

[35] Munawi, *Fayd al-Qadir*, 4/511; Ajluni, *Kashfu'l-Khafa*, 1/511

[36] *Ibid.*, 1/143

[37] Başar, Alaaddin, *Nur'dan Kelimeler- 2*, İstanbul: Zafer, 2000, pp. 160; 163

[38] *Sunan at-Tirmidhi*, Iman, 8; *Sunan ibn Majah*, Fitan, 12; Demircan, A. Rıza, *Süleymaniye Minberinden İslam Nizamı*, İstanbul: Ensar, 2008, pp. 104–109

ade the path of God is also *jihad*. However, in all of the above, the intention must be to please God.

The only thing that holds people back from performing *jihad* is their attachment to material life and its carnal pleasures. A grand duty such as *jihad* cannot be expected from a person who fails to give up comfort and make sacrifices from his personal pleasures. Expectations in this regard would be vain. Great missions could only be performed by those who make sacrifice from personal pleasures, both physical and spiritual.

In relation to those who cannot make these sacrifices and have no intentions to do so right from the beginning; we do not expect anything from them. All expectations aside, we would be concerned about the problems they would cause as soon as such people appear on stage. We do not believe that a person who has not given up on worldly pleasures to claim: "O God, sacrificing everything I own on Your path is really sweet" would make an effort in this regard or that his efforts would yield any fruits. The only people we believe in are the ones who have abandoned their selves, personal pleasures, homes and nations; people who have locked their doors and moved away like the Companions of the Prophet; people who have prevailed over the temptations of the flesh. Whatever we expect, we expect it from these people who are the very reason for God's aid.

The struggle that our people will undertake should be tailored to the teachings of the Qur'an. In this regard, the Holy Qur'an states:

> "O you who believe! What excuse do you have that when it is said to you: "Mobilize in God's cause!" you cling heavily to the earth? Are you content with the present, worldly life, rather than the Hereafter? Yet slight is the enjoyment of the worldly life as compared with the Hereafter. If you do not mobilize (as you are commanded), He will punish you grievously, and instead of you, He will substitute another people, and you will in no way harm Him. God has full power over everything. (at-Tawbah 9:38–39)

The Qur'an invites all believers to strive in God's cause. Consequently, our gain or lost (may God protect us) depends on our decision to accept or refuse this invitation. Either, like hypocrites, we will say, "Abandoning the pleasures of this life is a difficult task for us" or like the Companions, we will mobilize ourselves using everything we have.[39]

What Do the Terms *Tabligh, Irshad,* and *Amr bi al-Maruf, Nahy an al-Munkar* Mean?

Earlier we explained that the definition of *jihad* also included *tabligh,* conveying the virtues of faith to others, which means commanding of good and prevention of evil. Consequently, *tabligh* (conveyance), *irshad* (guidance) and *amr al-maruf* (enjoining good) is a form of *jihad.* Now, let us begin with *tabligh* and explain these concepts one by one:

The definition of *tabligh* is "to convey a message or report." In a religious context, it means taking all that is defined as good, blessed and virtuous by Islam to people of other nations and to inviting them to embrace these truths. In other words, it means explaining the truths and guiding people to the right path. The essence of *tabligh* is enjoining good and forbidding evil (*amr bi al-maruf wa nahy an al-munkar*). *Maruf* means "things that are commanded by religion" and *munkar* means "things that are prohibited by religion." We could also say that everything that is in accordance with the Qur'an and Sunnah can be described as *maruf* and everything that contradicts them, such as disbelief, unlawful acts and sins can be described as *munkar. Irshad,* on the other hand, can be defined as inviting and guiding people to righteousness so that they could attain contentment and happiness in their worldly lives and in the Hereafter. It is encouraging them to perform good deeds and warning them about evil deeds.

Tabligh and *Irshad* Are the Reason for the Creation of Human Beings

For every believer who has faith in God, *tabligh* has a close relationship with being considered as a true believer by the side of God and having the guarantee of remaining as a believer. Individuals and soci-

---

[39] Gülen, M. Fethullah, *I'la-yı Kelimetullah veya Cihad,* İzmir: Nil, 2001, p. 121

eties who believe in God can only continue their existence through the duty of *tabligh*. The reason for this is *tabligh* is the very purpose of our creation.

Living according to this purpose will salvage our worldly lives and the Hereafter. The following verse describes this reality quite evidently:

> There must be among you a community calling to good, and enjoining and actively promoting what is right, and forbidding and trying to prevent evil (in appropriate ways). They are those who are the prosperous. (Al Imran 3:104)

The alternative is explained grimly by our noble Prophet in the following *hadith*: "What will happen to you, on the day that people become rebellious and run on the streets indecently, the day that evil spreads all around you and conveying the truth is abandoned?"

Upon hearing this, the Companions of the Prophet became quite concerned because their minds could not comprehend the occurrence of such things. They believed that even if there was only one believer left in the world, this would be enough to stop the spreading of evil. For this reason the words of the Prophet had a deep affect on them. In shock, they asked: "Will this really occur, O Messenger of God?"

The Messenger of God replied: "By God, Who has my soul in His Power, what will occur is more severe than this."

There was a sense of confusion in the air hence they asked again in panic: "What could be worse than this O Messenger of God?"

Once again, the Prophet replied: "If you could only see yourselves on the day that evil is considered as good and good is considered as evil."

The Companions asked again in bafflement: "Will this occur too, O Messenger of God? Will people command evil and abolish good?"

"Even worse things will occur" replied the Prophet.

The Companions asked again: "What can be worse than this?"

The Messenger answered: "What will happen to you on the day you remain silent before evil and encourage it?"

By now the Companions were totally perplexed as they asked: "Will that happen too?"

The Prophet replied: "Something even worse will happen."

At this point the noble Messenger made a vow to God and conveyed a message from Him:

"I swear by My Grace, I will pour discord and dissension like a waterfall amongst a society that has fallen into such situation."[40]

Our noble Prophet was expressing the consequences of neglecting the duty of *tabligh* and its impact on the future of his *ummah* (community). In order to avoid such disaster, believers need to take on the responsibility of their original duty hence work vigorously and with the utmost eagerness.

"Humanity of this era is in need of *tabligh*, the commanding of good and prevention of evil more than ever. Prophethood has been concluded with our noble Prophet and this door has been closed for eternity. However, the amount of rebellion and disbelief in our time is equivalent to all periods of history. For this reason, those who take this Divine duty upon themselves will face more difficulties and burdens than the people of the past. It is because of these difficult conditions we believe and hope that people who are prepared to carry on the duty of spreading the virtues of faith in this day and age will surpass the people of the past and find the opportunity to take their honorable place right behind the Companions of the Messenger of God."[41]

READING TEXT

Fethullah Gülen Explains

A group of young men whose social status and ranks would draw the envy of anyone came to me with a list. These young men had not even taken a taste of life when all the pleasures of the world had been laid under their feet. The list contained some names and at the bottom there was a note which said:

---

[40] Haysami, *Macmau'z-Zevaid*, 7/280, 281
[41] Gülen, M. Fethullah, *İrşad Ekseni*, İzmir: Nil, 2001, p. 17

"For the love of God, pray for us so that we serve our religion and our people in every moment of our lives."

This describes the resurrection of the Companions of the Prophet. I prayed for them for a long time. I prayed so that their lives are spent on the path of religion. Without considering whether I deserved it or not, I included my own name at the end of the list. Using their names as an intercession, I beseeched a share from this Divine cause from the vast munificence of my Lord. The behavior and attitudes of these young people and thousands alike provides so much hope and prosperity that it trembles our hearts.

When we see them, our hopes lighten up and we say this will work. The reason we assume this is, now there are young people who carry the true meaning of this exalted cause deep in their hearts and represent it in accordance to its spiritual meaning and value. Yes, the numbers of those who go to bed with severe headaches have increased. Today, there are thousands of youth who feel the sorrow of disbelief and disbelievers in their hearts. Just like the Companions of the Prophet who formed the leading group, today we have a new generation who has sworn to undertake this duty; a generation attempting to display an effort that is equivalent to that of the Companions of the noble Messenger; emerging with fresh hope and new messages as they move with the scent of Prophet Muhammad, peace and blessings be upon him, and burn with desire to fulfill their mission as the way it should be done. We pray that our Lord do not demolish this movement because of our sins.[42]

Who Is the Most Blessed amongst Human Beings?

One day when our noble Prophet was sitting in the mosque, a man walked in and asked:

"Who is the most blessed amongst human beings?"

---

[42] Gülen, M. Fethullah, *Asrın Getirdiği Tereddütler-3,* İstanbul: Nil, 2011, p. 17

The Messenger of God replied: "The most blessed is the one who commands righteousness and prevents evil, recites the Qur'an a lot, fears God and visits his parents and relatives.[43]

The *hadith* explains that in order to become a believer whom God and His Messenger is pleased with, one needs to convey the message of God. This duty is more blessed than secluding into one corner and engaging in prayers. If this was not the case, our Prophet would have refrained from society and stayed in his house at all times to offer his prayers day and night. Therefore, if we wish to be amongst the most blessed people then we should use every opportunity to explain about our Lord to others.

By guiding other people to the right path we get the chance to earn rewards as much as the number of people who have embraced our faith. Let us explain the issue more meticulously: for instance, a believer has encouraged his friend to perform good deeds. In such a case, the same amount of spiritual rewards earned by the friend who performs good deeds will also be earned by the person who has guided him, without any decrease in the rewards. Our noble Prophet states: "A person, who causes something good or teaches a good deed to someone else, will be considered as if he has performed this deed himself."[44]

As it is clear by the *hadith*, taking even the smallest step on this path earns great rewards hence it signifies the importance of performing "enjoining good and forbidding evil."

Tabligh and *Irshad* Are the Duties of a Believer

In relation to this, our Lord cautions us with the following verse:

> The believers, both men and women: they are guardians, confidants, and helpers of one another. They enjoin and promote what is right and good, and forbid and try to prevent the evil, and they establish the Prescribed Prayer in conformity with its conditions, and pay the Prescribed Purifying Alms. They obey God and His Messenger. They are the ones whom God will treat with mercy. Surely God is All-Glorious with irresistible might, All-Wise. (at-Tawbah 9:71)

---

[43] Ahmad ibn Hanbal, *Al-Musnad*, 6/432
[44] *Sunan at-Tirmidhi*, Ilim, 14

The verse explains to us that it is the duty of a believer to encourage his brother in good deeds and discourage him from evil. This responsibility is described by the verse as being part of a believer's inseparable disposition.

Why is this duty so important? The answer to the question is: in order to attain a harmonious and peaceful society, its members need to be distanced from malevolence. Malevolence resembles a virus. Unless, it is treated in time, it will spread to the entire body. In turn, the body will eventually be paralyzed. It is the spreading of small sins, which appear to be harmless at the beginning, has always caused the destruction of societies.

In a *hadith*, our noble Prophet indicates to this reality: "When someone saw another person committing an evil act, he would say "O such and such person, this is not *halal* so you should stop doing this act!" However, when he came back the next day, he would see that the man has not given up on the evil act, yet he would continue his friendship with him; he would eat and drink with him. It is because of this behavior, God made their hearts similar."

He also says: "By God, you must command the good and forbid evil and certainly, you must hold the tyrant by the hand and bring him onto the path of righteousness."[45]

As the *hadith* explains the situation of some people in the past who handed out a visa for evil deeds, it also warns Muslims about such consequences and the way they should be prevented. Consequently, we could say that *irshad* and *tabligh* are two imperatives that act as a lightning rod which protects societies from total destruction. For as long as there is commanding of good and prevention of evil within a society, God will not send calamity to such people.

Our noble Prophet explains this in the following *hadith*: "The situation of those who fulfill the commandments of God and those who refuse, resemble the situation of people traveling together on the same boat. Some of these people travel on the top deck while others travel at the bottom. If the people at the lower deck who need water but do

---

[45] *Sunan Abu Dawud*, Melahim, 17; *Sunan ibn Majah*, Fitan, 20

not wish to discomfort those travelling at the top decide to puncture a hole on the floor and the people at the top turn a blind eye to this, they would all sink."[46]

Taking this *hadith* as an example, we could say that the entire world is a boat that resembles the Noah's Ark. Entire humanity has no other option but to travel on this boat. Indeed, the boat we call earth is unique hence there is no other like it. It is the duty of every human being to protect this boat from sinking and look after it with care. This is a duty bestowed upon us from the time we board this boat.

As we need to protect the society from evil that resembles a poisonous vermin such as a snake or a scorpion, we also need to equip the society with virtues such as good behavior, good manners and morals. A society composed of individuals who possess pure hearts will refrain from all evil. This is one aspect of the issue; the other is the matter of allowing the medium for the flourishing good things within the society. This is the duty we have undertaken for the future of our society. This is a sanctified mission, and it is difficult and burdensome as much as it is sacred.[47]

READING TEXT
Owning up to Religion Is a Primary Obligation upon All Believers

In this day and age, supporting religion which means spreading its message is a primary obligation for all believers. No believer is excluded from this imperative duty. Indeed, all believers must learn their religion and put it into practice in their daily lives. And then, they should explain their experiences to others so that the world of others could also be illuminated with *nur* (Divine light).

In all periods of history there have been people who are in need of guidance. Believers traveling on the same boat with those who are wasting their lives in the valleys of misguidance thus looking for a way out, are obligated to fulfill their responsibilities towards their co-

---

[46] *Sahih al-Bukhari*, Sharika, 6
[47] Gülen, M. Fethullah, *İrşad Ekseni*, İzmir: Nil, 2001, pp. 69–70

travelers. Besides being a mission given by God himself, this duty is also a prerequisite of being human. Depending on their status, level and means available, everyone has an obligation towards this duty. Otherwise, being accountable for this duty on the Day of Judgment will be a difficult task.

When we scrutinize the history, we will see that those who have undertaken this noble duty of invitation and guidance have always followed the same path.[48] After receiving this noble duty, the Messenger of God spent every day of his life conveying the message of religion. He would travel door to door looking for a friendly face and a heart to convey his message.

Initially, no one showed any consideration or interest. Later, some began to ridicule him. Gradually, their attitudes turned to harassment, insult and torture. They were laying thorns on his path and pouring the internal organs of dead animals down his head as he stood for the Prayer. They believed that it was ok to torture and harass the Messenger of God in all forms of manner. However, contrary to all attacks, the noble Messenger did not give an inch and never felt wearisome of his duty, because this was the very reason for his existence. He visited everyone repeatedly, including his archenemies. He conveyed the Divine message. Who knows how many times he visited Abu Jahl and Abu Lahab, archenemies of Islam and faith, and delivered the message of Islam to them! He was walking around the fairs and visiting all the tents with an intention to save the faith of one person. Wherever he went, doors would be shut on his face yet he would go again and again with the same message.

As Mecca became an unlivable place for the noble Messenger, he migrated to Medina. He was to spread his Divine light in this city now.

He did not stay away from his duty of invitation and guidance, not even for a moment. He explained religion to the smallest detail and invited people to it. Throughout his stay in Medina, even during the conflicts, he did not withdraw from conveying his message to every individual.

---

[48] Gülen, M. Fethullah, *İ'la-yı Kelimetullah veya Cihad,* İzmir: Nil, 2001, p. 7

Our noble Messenger was a unique individual who carried the weighty obligation of Prophethood on his shoulders for twenty-three years, fulfilling his responsibilities like no other man of action.[49]

What Kind of a *Tabligh* Strategy Should a Young Person Follow?

As mentioned before, each Muslim, young and old has an obligation to pass on the message of God and His Messenger to those around them. This is a duty of utmost priority for all believers. It is for this Divine reason and wisdom that the Prophets were sent. Consequently, we have also been blessed with carrying on this noble duty. In this regard, service is a race of virtue. Those who serve on this path are the most virtuous people on earth.

In this day and age, ideologies and perspectives have been distanced from faith. In fact, faith has been pushed out of daily life. Science and technology are presented as enemies of religion and society is deceived. For this reason, Islam, the Qur'an and issues related to faith should be learned thoroughly and then these Divine lights should be explained to others slowly and with ease.

Every job has a certain technique that is exclusive to it. It is impossible to talk about a scientific discipline in the absence of a technique or a method. Since this is the reality, invitation to virtue and prevention of evil is the most important discipline and a duty for all believers hence this noble duty also has a certain technique and methodology.

In order to fulfill this duty, one needs to take great care with certain principles. Let us now try to summarize these principles:

1. ONE SHOULD HAVE BROAD KNOWLEDGE IN RELIGIOUS MATTERS

A person of *tabligh* should possess extensive knowledge about his own faith and religion before he could explain it to others. Otherwise, grave mistakes can be made in the name of religion and those who are doing

---

[49] Gülen, M. Fethullah, *Sonsuz Nur-1*, İstanbul: Nil, 2007, pp. 61–62

the invitation can frighten people away from religion and themselves. Initially, one should have comprehensive knowledge on the Qur'an, the Book of God. Along with the text of the Qur'an, one should also learn about its meaning and spirit. In this regard, one should refer to the interpretation and exegesis of the Qur'an. In addition to this, the life of our noble Prophet and the lives of his Companions should be studied through *hadith* narrations and history of Islam. Finally, one should study *ilmihal* (the basics of the Islamic faith) and books that will help him gather the necessary information which he aims to convey to others.

In relation to Islamic knowledge, we have two main sources: the Qur'an and Sunnah. When explaining religion to others, one should remain within the principles of these two sources and possess comprehensive knowledge about them. We should digest the topics that we will explain to others, so well that the people we address could also be nourished with ease.

We should be like sheep when we feed others, not like birds which feed their young with spew. We should process what we learned and convert it into milk and let it flow into the needy hearts like a water of life, a fountain of remedy. Through such method, this information will enter their hearts and produce a honey comb and honey in the name of wisdom and knowledge.

Of course, this could only occur through reading and understanding and also through the expansion of our culture and knowledge. For this reason, those who have taken on the duty of invitation to the universal virtues must reserve a certain part of their day to reading. A person who is deprived of the culture of his era will have nothing to offer to today's society. In other words, a person who has insufficient knowledge about culture will not be able to satisfy the person addressed for too long. Consequently, a person who is in contact with people of all levels must possess enough knowledge to satisfy his audience.

Indeed, those who have made *irshad* (invitation and guidance to virtues) an objective of their lives must be well equipped with the necessary knowledge. The words of an empty person will also be empty. Moreover, such people who have nothing to offer will try to cover up their ignorance with rage and violence. In reaction to such conduct, people they address will refuse to accept even the most logical and simple issues.

2. THE SCIENCE AND TECHNOLOGY OF THE CURRENT ERA SHOULD BE STUDIED IN DETAIL

In modern times, perspective on worldly life and analysis of occurrences and matter has completely changed. We live in times where reason and logic have more weight. People who are in need of faith speak through the tongue of science and philosophy. In response, Muslims should also be speaking with modern science and technology. This can only be realized through a comprehensive knowledge of the current era. In a way, this could be considered as true knowledge and wisdom. Moreover, knowledge and wisdom are inseparable qualities of a believer.

The people of *irshad*, in this day and age must have knowledge, even if it is in the form of encyclopedic knowledge. Otherwise, their invitation to virtues would not include everyone, but it will be restricted to a private talk. Those who are oblivious of the era they are living in are in actual fact living in a dark abyss. The invitation of such people will be quite ineffective. Furthermore, the grindstone of time and conditions will eventually render them completely ineffective. For this reason, a Muslim should convey his message in parallel to the day and age he is living in.

3. WE MUST LOOK FOR DIFFERENT WAYS TO ENTER THE HEARTS OF PEOPLE

Primarily, one should look for ways to enter into the heart of his addressee. This is the humanitarian way of approaching the issue. Notions such as exchanging gifts and solving problems should be put into practice since they are the actions which were commanded to us through the spirit of religion.

We need to look for every legitimate way to enter the heart of our addressee; hence the person to whom we will explain the virtues of faith must first have complete trust in our friendship. This is an important factor which has an impact on the things we will explain and thus it should never be neglected.

4. AS WE EXPLAIN THE ISSUES, WE NEED TO TAKE THE AUDIENCE'S LEVEL OF KNOWLEDGE INTO CONSIDERATION

Dropping down to the level of our audience when explaining the issues is a Divine manner. Our noble Prophet invites us to follow the ethics of God. The Qur'an is a Divine Word, which was brought down to the level of human comprehension.

In this day and age, youth have become estranged to religious terms and expressions. We need to speak to them through a language they understand. Just as the way we walk with a three year old toddler as we hold his hand, smile and behave like him as we interact, we should also take into consideration the level of our audience when we make *tabligh*.

5. WE SHOULD REFRAIN FROM DISPUTES AND ARGUMENTS

During one-on-one talks, we should be extremely careful that the discussion is not turned into a dispute. The reason for this is, during disputes and arguments it is conceit and arrogance that speaks instead of the truth. So, no matter how logical or rational we speak during an argument, our words will have no effect.

From a psychological perspective, it will be unreasonable to assume that an argument or a dispute could unearth the truth, because, as we prepare for an argument we plan our strategy on how to defeat our opponent, just as they make plans to defeat us. Therefore, our opponent will bring counter arguments to all the evidence we provide hence the dispute will transform into a vicious cycle that will never be resolved even if the discussions continue for days.

6. WE NEED TO EARN THE TRUST OF OUR ADDRESSEE

The person you are inviting to religion should trust you to the extent that if he was to put in a situation where he needs to make a choice between you and all the things he loves, you should come first. The reason for this is your relationship with him is based solely on the love of God. Since you love this person for the sake of God only, this love will have an effect in his heart. Your influence should be so powerful that he should choose the heavy responsibilities which he would take on by just being with you over all the pleasures he would receive by being on the other side. Moreover, all the difficulties and dangers he may face by being on the ideal path that you have dedicated yourself to should be more attractive to him than the pleasures and comforts of his previous lifestyle. This can only be achieved through the recognition and trust he feels towards you.

7. WE NEED TO BE LOGICAL AND REALISTIC

A person of *tabligh* is a person of sound reason. He should try to convince his audience by presenting his explanations in accordance to the level of his audience and in a reasonable way. He should evaluate situations using the same method of reason. The acceptance of the words of a person of *tabligh* by the society depends on his ability of reasoning hence this ability will also protect him from being ridiculed. Here is an impressive example from the noble Prophet: Julaybib was a young man who had a weakness towards women. One day, he approached the Prophet and said, "O Messenger of God, give me permission to commit adultery." The Companions of the Prophet tried to silence him as they asked him to be quite. But the noble Prophet said, "Come sit next to me." Julaybib came and sat next to the Prophet. The Prophet than asked him: "Would you want someone to commit adultery with your mother?"

"By God! I would never wish this!" replied Julaybib.

"Of course, no one would want their mothers to commit adultery. How about your daughter? Would you want someone to commit adultery with her?" asked the Messenger of God.

"O Messenger of God; of course I would not want this either," replied Julaybib.

The noble Prophet then said: "No one would wish this either. How about your aunty? Would you wish this upon her?"

Julaybib replied: "No, O Messenger of God, of course not!"

"No one would wish such a thing, then you must understand that the women you intent to commit adultery with are all someone's mother, daughter, sister or aunty," said the Messenger of God.

The Prophet had already made his pointed as he placed his hand on the chest of this young man and prayed: "O God! Forgive his sins, purify his heart and protect his chastity."[50]

It is recorded that following the prayer, Julaybib became a symbol of modesty.

READING TEXT
How Did the Noble Prophet Gain the Trust of the People?

Here is a beautiful example from the Age of Happiness: Utba ibn Walid was one of the wealthiest people in Mecca. He was also one of the archenemies of the noble Prophet. Whenever, there was a devious plot prepared against the noble Prophet, he would be involved. He was the leader of the rebellion waged against God. There was a young man raised in the home of this unfortunate man, he was the son of Utba and he was nothing like his father. He made his pledge to the noble Messenger of God and so with the back of his hand he pushed aside everything his father placed in front of him in the name of worldly pleasures.

The name of this young man was Huzayfa. His father had laid his entire wealth in front of him so that he may turn away from the Messenger of God. However, with the lessons he learnt from his noble teacher and mentor, Huzayfa had developed a solid faith and conviction. Previously, when they came to God's Messenger with a similar offer, he had replied: "If you place the sun in my right hand and the earth in the other, I will not turn away from my cause!" His words had found such an effect in the hearts and souls of the Companions that the offer made to Huzayfa was going to receive the same reply.

---

[50] Ahmad ibn Hanbal, *Al-Musnad*, 4/420–421; Haysami, *Majmau'z-zawaid*, 9/368

Their sanctified teacher had entered their hearts in such a way that he would inhabit their souls for eternity.

Since the time of the noble Prophet, the method of *tabligh*, invitation to religion has not changed. Although the conditions of that particular era were a little different to modern age, everything else remains the same. This means that the guides and teachers of today should follow the method of the noble Prophet in regards to winning the hearts of people. Otherwise, the issues conveyed to people will not have any effect hence they will not be accepted.

This is the name of a strategy which consists of touching the souls and entering the hearts. One should contemplate on the fact that if God's Messenger had not attracted the love of his Companions so extensively; would they have followed him to the battle of Badr? Every now and then he would speak to them and drive into their hearts the notion of choosing him over anything else.

For example: he reprimanded Ka'b ibn Malik for falling back during the battle of Tabuq as he asked him: "Did you not give me your word at Aqaba? Were you not going to follow me wherever I go? Ka'b did not deny any of this as he replied: "Yes, O Messenger of God; I gave you my word! I had never prepared myself for battle conditions in such way before. However, I kept on delaying it by thinking, "I shall leave the next day." Finally, I left home but could not catch up with you." He was asking for forgiveness from the Messenger of God. Since he was telling the truth and displaying his loyalty with a sincere attitude, he was forgiven.

This is the way a guide should enter the hearts of his pupils. His expectations from his followers should only be for the sake of God. This means that he should never expect something for himself. According to the Holy Qur'an, the situation of those who request something for themselves are similar to the situation of pharaohs, Nimrud and Shaddad. On the other hand, the Messenger of God had always made a request in the name of God and for the wellbeing of his people. This is another topic that should be approached with extreme sensitivity.

8. EVERYTHING SHOULD BE DONE WITH
SINCERITY AND EARNESTNESS

Intentions should always contain the aim of pleasing God and everything should be organized according to this. Every project or activity must be evaluated from the perspective of earning the pleasure of God and if the project is going to please God then it should be realized, otherwise, it should be abandoned. One should not allow a medium where people would be deceived or disillusioned.

This is clearly explained in a *hadith*: Musa al Ashari narrates: They asked the noble Messenger of God: "Three men go to battle, one to protect the honor of his nation and family, the other to display his courage and the third to make a name for himself. Which one is on the path of God?" The noble Prophet replied: "Whoever struggles on the path to exalting the Name of God, he is on the path of God."[51]

With this *hadith*, God's Messenger restricts the definition of *jihad* to a struggle done on the path to spreading the religion of God. This means that if there is a struggle made on the path to spreading the exalted Name of God, this is done for the sake of God. Otherwise, we would only be promoting ourselves hence there will be no sign of sincerity or spiritual rewards in such deeds. One cannot talk about the pleasure of God or entering into the hearts of others in such attempts where sincerity has been damaged so extensively.

Those who came before us have fulfilled this mission with sincerity. There were such people amongst them that when they uttered a perfect word, they would prostrate and make the following prayer: "O God, do not take me away from sincerity." People like Umar ibn Abdulaziz would tear up the letter he had written when he realized that it was too perfect in literature. He would then write another letter which was simpler in context of literature. He did this because he wished to abstain from conceit and arrogance.

Indeed, sincerity and earnestness are the soul and heart of the issues explained above. If we do not want people to ridicule what he

---

[51] *Sahih al-Bukhari*, Ilim, 45; Jihad, 15; Tawhid, 28; *Sahih Muslim*, Imara, 150, 151

have explained to them, then we must hold onto sincerity and do it steadfastly.

9. SOMETIMES IT MAY BE NECESSARY TO LET OTHERS EXPLAIN THE TOPIC

If there is a topic that may cause a reaction or a negative response when we make the explanation, then we should say, "The sake of God is more exalted" and we should let someone else explain the topic. Moreover, we should do this with satisfaction. There is a fine detail here. Acceptance of the explanation made by someone else is different to being pleased with it. We should be in the second category where we should be pleased and this is something that the carnal soul does not like. Furthermore, this is an act of gallantry.

There may be some individuals who display a negative reaction to our explanations due to an issue related to our character. In this case, everything we explain will have a negative effect on them. Insisting on explaining God and the truth of religion to such people would be same as encouraging them to reject the truth. As a result, they will at a lost for refusing to accept the truth and we will be guilty for being an obstacle on the path of the truth. The solution to this problem is letting someone else explain the issues to such people. On the other hand, by learning from someone else, they will benefit from accepting the truth and we will be rewarded for our contribution. For this reason, the best person to explain an issue should be organized and we should not feel any discomfort when we listen with others in the audience.

10. WHEN WE ARE FACED WITH A TOPIC WE DO NOT KNOW, WITH EASE, WE SHOULD SAY "I DO NOT KNOW"

In this regard, our noble guide, the Messenger of God is the best example for us. The Jewish scholars were asking him a question about the spirit. He would not answer them until a revelation came down. Once he received the revelation, he answered them.

What did he say when the angel of revelation, Gabriel came to him and asked about the time of the doomsday? He replied: "In relation to this issue, I have no more knowledge than the person who is asking the question." Is there a better example which teaches us the following principle: We do not have to answer every question put forward to us?

They asked a hundred questions to Imam Abu Yusuf. He replied to sixty of these questions by saying, "I do not know." Then they said to him, "O Imam, we pay you a salary yet from the one hundred questions we asked, you replied, "I do not know" to most of them. How is this possible?" The great Imam replied, "You pay me for the things that I know. If you had to pay for the things I do not know, the entire wealth of the world would not be enough." Those days, Imam Abu Yusuf held the highest rank in the office of providing *fatwa*.

These examples prove that even the highest ranked spiritual leaders did not provide answers to all questions. Moreover, they replied comfortably by saying "I do not know." We too should say we do not know when we really do not know. However, we should follow up the issue by referring the person who asked the question to someone who knows the answer. As we make an effort to learn ourselves, we should also provide the medium for others to learn as well.

11. WE SHOULD FIRST PRACTICE WHAT WE PREACH

One of the utmost important principles of *tabligh* is "Preach what you practice and practice what you preach." The reason for this is that a person of *tabligh* is an individual who has dedicated himself to becoming a genuine believer. Moreover, a person of *tabligh* should be in the realization of the fact that words without practice will have no effect on hearts. God Almighty will not bless or create an effect for words and actions that does not contain sincerity.

A person of *tabligh* should be extremely cautious in regard to this issue. When he is alone, he should behave in the same manner as he displays when he is with others. Furthermore, he should try to be sincere in all of his actions and activities displayed in both out in the open and in privacy.

A *tabligh* performed with the tongue only, by people who do not take on the manners of Islam, who do not adhere to Sunnah and by people who perform their Prayers with insolence, yawning and bulging, is in fact can be considered as murder. Islam is a religion which the entire humanity longs for but cannot attain. If those who invite people to the pure, simple and natural life style of Islam continue to sit back in their comfortable armchairs and indulge themselves in the luxuries of eating and drinking through fantasies, their invitees will say: "Why don't you first live the Islamic lifestyle which you describe as pure and simple. Only then we shall follow you."

Indeed, the only path to entering the hearts of others is to follow the noble Prophet's system and methodology by first practicing what you preach.

12. A PERSON OF *TABLIGH* SHOULD BE BENEVOLENT

A person of *tabligh* should be prepared to sacrifice everything he possesses in life. On the path of winning the hearts of others, he should transform his munificence into a *Buraq* (the noble Prophet's ride on the night of the Ascension) and continue his journey in this way. When we mention the word "munificence" we remember our mother Khadija. She was born long before our noble Prophet and died before him. Perhaps coming earlier and leaving early came to her from her name. The name Khadija means "born premature." When she met the Messenger of God, he had nothing in the name of this world. On the other hand, Khadija was a wealthy noble woman who was also very pretty. However, this did not keep her away from realizing the great meaning which the Prophet possessed hence this woman of insight aspired him. She was a business woman who organized trade caravans. She had children from the noble Messenger. However, she did not live to see the era of Medina. She reunited with her Lord, the All-Merciful God, before the Hijra.

She was created in a unique way and this made her an appropriate wife for a Prophet. This great woman was indeed genuinely benevolent. As the noble Prophet commenced his duty as the Messenger of God, she confirmed him immediately without any hesitation as if she knew that he would be given this duty. Then she placed all her wealth under the control of the noble Messenger. This great wealth was spent on the path of God. During the time when the polytheists of Mecca applied a boycott against Muslims, this great wealth of Khadija had finished. They were in such situation that on some occasions the noble Prophet almost fell unconscious due to starvation. They could not find anything to eat. They were deprived of even a morsel of dried bread. It was during this period, Khadija became ill and they did not even have the means to look for a cure. Under these grief-stricken circumstances, our mother flew away towards the eternal life. The very limit of benevolence is the moment when you lose everything hence our mother Khadija had reached this limit before anyone.

Abu Bakr on the other hand was distracting his father with the pebble stones he had placed in a jar whilst he spent all of his gold coins on the path of God. For this reason, even when he became the Caliph, he would milk the sheep of others to earn a living. Not long ago, he was one of the wealthiest businessmen in Mecca. This loyal friend of the Messenger of God who accompanied him in the cave had also displayed his munificence as he gave everything away on the path of God. Umar ibn Khattab was no different. He lived a life similar to the poorest person in Medina, surviving on a few dates. This meant that he had spent all of his wealth on this path as well.

In this regard, all the Companions where in fact competing with each other. The benevolence they displayed in the cause of what they believed won the hearts of many people. Just as they did with every issue, they learned this from the noble Messenger of God as well. One day, a man went to his people and said: "O my people! Submit to this person, because he is the Messenger of God. He would not be so generous if he wasn't, thus he would fear poverty. But, he gives everyone whatever they ask of him."

Young and old, everyone should use these methods to enter the hearts of others and to conquer their souls. If a person spends all of his wealth to save the faith of one individual, he would be at a great gain and at no lost at all.

The doors of Paradise will be opened by the generous. We need to clear the path that leads to these doors so that we could take many others with us. The first people to enter Paradise will not be scholars, imams or preachers but it will be those fortunate souls who spent their wealth and years on the path to explaining the truths of faith.

13. WE SHOULD BE INSISTENT, RELENTLESS AND WE SHOULD NEVER GIVE UP

Being persistent in *tabligh* is a means to earn the approval of God. At the same time, this persistency is a sign of sincerity and a key for the acceptance of what is explained. Persistence is a clear indication of being aware of the significance and sensitivity of the issues explained. In other words: The Almighty God gives great importance to the declaration of "There is no deity but God" and He wants this sentence to reside in the hearts of human beings. For this reason, a person of *tabligh* dedicates his life to this mission which has great significance by the side of God and works vigorously to place this declaration of God's Oneness and Unity into the hearts of all human beings. Through such action, the person of *tabligh* gives an appropriate response to the cause valued so highly by God. Indeed, persistency in *tabligh* carries such an important meaning.

This means that the person of Hizmet shows persistency in things considered as important by God. This in turn will show the level of his sincerity in his arguments. A person, who has not dedicated his life to things he believes, cannot be a true guide. Such people cannot even be dubbed as guides. A guide must explain his topic a hundred times over and if no one listens to him then he should say, "This is the 101st" and explain it again. He should wait for the right occasion and the instant where he will be most effective. He should continue to explain throughout his life, without sulking and huffing. Just like the Prophets who never gave up. The lives of the Prophets consist of persistency. Yes, they conveyed the message of God with perseverance.

14. THE RESULT SHOULD BE LEFT TO GOD

Those who are in the business of *tabligh* should always leave the result to God hence they should never intervene in the results. It is their duty to convey the message, but the results are up to the Almighty God.

People who invite others to religion should only think of their duties. There were Prophets in history who conveyed their message throughout their lives but not even one person believed in them. This did not deter them in anyway hence they continued to fulfill their mission without showing any sign of dissuasion. In no part of their lives did they ever show opposition by arguing: "Why couldn't I serve?" "Why doesn't anyone believe me?" "Why wasn't this mission successful?" Yes, they never lost hope and they never complained.

Every Prophet thinks solely about their mission. For this reason, they prepare themselves for all situations and conditions and then get on with their missions. Forcing people to accept their message is not a part of their duty. In this regard, the verdict belongs to God only.[52]

READING TEXT
Guidelines for the People of Service

- Our noble Prophet has only been to Hajj once in his life. His entire life has passed by means of inviting others to virtues and guiding them.
- Some tears can conquer many hearts.
- Greatness and great achievements cannot be found in great plans but they could be found in seeking the pleasure of God, and His approval.
- Do not delay planting your seeds until the harvest season, because your efforts for both seasons will be in vain.
- A believer must place his faith on the foundations of practice. When faith and practice apply a pressure on one's emotions, it defines a path for his behavior.
- If a person is distressed by his mistakes, then he knows the difference between a good deed and sin.
- Comfort and luxury are the enemies of success. Muslims can only succeed by living a simple life.

---

[52] Gülen, M. Fethullah, *Sonsuz Nur-1*, İstanbul: Nil, 2007, pp. 162–164; Gülen, M. Fethullah, *İrşad Ekseni*, İzmir: Nil, 2001, p. 134–140; Gülen, M. Fethullah, *Asrın Getirdiği Tereddütler-3*, İstanbul: Nil, 2011, pp. 17–20

- Even if precaution does not change destiny, it protects one from accusing destiny.

- The most important issue in *tabligh* is its connection to sincerity and its acceptance by the addressee. No one should make *tabligh* to those who are at a higher level than themselves because it can cause an opposite result. A son to his father, student to his teacher and an apprentice to his master, should not explain anything. Abu Talib's refusal to accept our noble Prophet is an important matter for consideration.

- Believers are the representatives of security and trust on earth.

- Evil can be prevented by behaving humanly towards those who have locked themselves onto evil. The principle of "A human being is a slave of kindness" should not be forgotten.

- Most times, the devil will lead astray those who do not live their lives by focusing on invitation and guidance. Those who do not call to good and prevent evil will be deprived from the blessings of Divine revelation. Such people can never be a source of inspiration. They may even write books but their work will bear no fruits. Those who invite to good and prevent from evil will always be a source of inspiration. In order to keep our hearts and souls dynamic, we need to read, contemplate and try to explain something to everyone.

- The purpose of all guides should be to earn the pleasure of God, hence worldly emotions and feelings should never be an objective for them. A true guide should think along these lines: "One day, if my path crosses through Hell, even there, I will look for a familiar face to whom I could explain my cause." This is the portrait of a man of service who we long for in this day and age.[53]

QUESTIONS

1. Which one of the below describes "enjoining good and forbidding evil"?

[53] Gülen, M. Fethullah, *Ölçü veya Yoldaki Işıklar*, İstanbul: Nil, 2011, pp. 208–211

a) *Tafakkur*

b) *Tazakkur*

c) *Amr bi al-maruf wa nahy an al-munkar*

d) *Salah*

2. Which one describes the term "removing obstacles from between the servants and God?"

a) *Salah*

b) *Jihad*

c) *Adhan*

d) *Dua*

3. Which of the below is not a principle of *tabligh*?

a) Having comprehensive knowledge about religious issues

b) Having knowledge about scientific and technological developments

c) Doing everything with sincerity and earnestness

d) When there is a question you do not know the answer to, you do not need to say "I do not know."

4. Which of the below is wrong in relation to *tabligh*?

a) *Tabligh* and guidance are the ongoing duties of a believer.

b) *Tabligh* and guidance are a priority above all obligations in this day and age.

c) *Tabligh* and guidance can only be done with the support of the government.

d) We should be respectful to people of all faiths when we make *tabligh*.

5. Which of the below describes abstaining from sins, observing the obligatory acts by taking the carnal soul under control, behaving according to the Sunnah of the noble Prophet and making an effort to explain everything that one learns about the truths of faith to relatives and everyone in the community?

a) The greater *jihad*

b) The lesser *jihad*

c) Contemplation

d) Remembering death

6. Which of the word definition below is wrong?
   a) *Munkar*: Things seen as repulsive by Islam
   b) *Kalima at-tawhid*: La ilaha illa'Allah
   c) *Salah*: The Prayer
   d) *Hizmet*: Selfishness

7. Who made the following statement? "As we need to protect the society from evil that resembles a poisonous vermin such as a snake or a scorpion, we also need to equip the society with virtues such as good behavior, good manners and morals."
   a) M. Fethullah Gülen
   b) Yahya Kemal Beyatlı
   c) Bediüzzaman Said Nursi
   d) Mehmet Akif Ersoy

8. "Our noble Prophet performed Hajj once in his entire life. However, he spent his life performing *irshad and tabligh*." What is the main theme in this statement?
   a) The importance of invitation to universal virtues and guidance
   b) One should not perform Hajj more than once.
   c) Although the noble Prophet wished he could perform Hajj more than once, he could not.
   d) Hajj is a very important form of worship.

9. In some languages the term *jihad* is defined as "Holy War." Is this a correct definition? Why?
   a) It is correct because Islam commands war.
   b) It is correct because *jihad* is a Holy War.
   c) It is incorrect because *jihad* does not only mean war but it encompasses every effort made on the path of spreading virtues.
   d) It is incorrect because *jihad* means peace.

10. Which of the below cannot be an objective of *jihad*?
    a) Taking the name of God to people
    b) Raising the banner of truth
    c) Removing the obstacles between human beings and God
    d) Conquering lands for their wealth and resources

3

REPRESENTATION: THE TONGUE OF CONDUCT

"Muslim's language used in the process of conveying the truths of religion to others should be the tongue of conduct rather than his physical tongue."[54] (M. Fethullah Gülen)

What is Representation and Tongue of Conduct?

Representation and the tongue of conduct means an invitation to religion made by a person of *tabligh* through his/her behavior and good conduct; it is displaying a role model behavior by practicing what is preached. Representation is one the best methods of explaining the truths of religion. One should practice what he attempts to explain to others, at a level which he has benefitted from them. This is an important factor in *tabligh*.

True gallantry is in representation. A person who has dedicated himself to explaining the truths of the Qur'an and faith cannot live a life that is contradictory to the realities he explains. Positive behavior and good conduct should be role modeled by those who promote them so that they could have an effect on others. What this means is, a person explaining the Daily Prayers should first offered them himself so that others could say, "Even if this person does not have anything else going for him, his Prayers are enough to prove that he is on the right path." Moreover, even if people do not accept him completely, they should at least believe that Prayers should be taken seriously.

---

[54] Gülen, M. Fethullah, "Allah'ım bizi kendimize getir," Kırık Testi, http://tr.fgulen.com/content/view/12100/9/

The blessed souls who have undertaken the duty of *irshad* and *tabligh* must first practice what they preach. In this regard, the Holy Qur'an cautions us with the following verse: *"Do you enjoin upon people godliness and virtue but forget your own selves, (even) while you recite the Book (and see therein the orders, prohibitions, exhortations and warnings)? Will you not understand and come to your senses?"* (al-Baqarah 2:44). *"O you who believe! Why do you say what you do not do (as well as what you will not do)? Most odious it is in the sight of God that you say what you do not (and will not) do"* (as-Saf 61:2–3).

In one *hadith*, our noble Prophet explains this issue with the following words: "Those who command righteousness to others but forget themselves shall drag their intestines in the hellfire. When they are asked, 'Who are you?' They will reply, 'We are those who commanded righteousness to others but forgot ourselves.'"[55]

The words and attitude of a person of *tabligh* should complete each other, he should take extreme care in not showing any weakness in his representation and he should first practice what he preaches.

For the Noble Prophet, Representation Came before *Tabligh*

When we analyze the Prophet's life, we see that role modeling was always one step ahead of *tabligh*. He would role model the matters he explained so sensitively that those who observed him would believe in God without having a need for further proof. There were many cases in which people accepted his Prophethood by just looking at him. Abdullah ibn Rawaha says, "Even if he had not come with clear miracles, one look at him would have been enough to believe." [56] What a wonderful way of explaining the truth.

The noble Prophet's representation was so effective that a Jewish scholar, Abdullah ibn Salam embraced Islam with a glance upon his

---

[55] As-Suyuti, *Ad-Durru'l-Mansur*, 1/158
[56] Kadi Iyad, *Ash-Shifa*, 1/249

face. He said: "There is no lie on this face. Only a Messenger of God can possess such a face."[57]

This means that seeing him was enough to accept him. Those who have dedicated their lives to explaining something to others will know the difficulty of such rapid acceptance. Most of these people work vigorously throughout their lives but cannot find a handful of followers or encourage people to accept their religion by entering their hearts. On the other hand, let us take a look at our noble Prophet. Can you show another person who has established his throne in the hearts of more than one billion people? Or is there another person whose name is chanted out five times a day from the minarets with great excitement and a sound that echoes all over the world?

This means, humanity loves him hence declare their loyalty continuously each day on a number of occasions. Contrary to all, the noble Prophet continues to enter the hearts of people, because he practiced what he preached to others and became a perfect role model for humanity. For this reason, everything he said found a place in the hearts of people and was accepted by nations.

As he invited people to servanthood and obedience to God, he represented this servanthood in its purest form by praying throughout the night until his feet were swollen. One day, he was reminded that all of his past and future sins were already forgiven and asked why he was placing so many burdens upon himself. He replied: "Should I not be a thankful servant?"[58]

If he wished, he could have lived like the kings. Such life of self indulgence was already offered to him in Mecca. However, for the sake of his religion, he preferred a life of hardship to a life of luxury. It was this simple life style that attracted many people to him.

His Caliph, Umar ibn Khattab also lived a very simple life. Yet the life of the Prophet would always bring tears to Umar's eyes. One day, the noble Messenger asked him why he was weeping. Umar replied, "O Messenger of God, as the kings of the world sleep in their bird-

---

[57] Aliyyulqari, *Al-Masnu'*, 149
[58] Ibn Hibban, *Sahih*, 2/386

feathered beds now, you sleep on a mat made up of straws. It has made marks on your body. You are the Messenger of God and you deserve a comfortable life more than anyone!" The noble Messenger replied, "O Umar, aren't you satisfied with the world being theirs but the Hereafter ours?"[59]

Yes, he lived a life of simplicity. In other words we could say that he did not live but he let others live. His secret in entering the souls of others lied within the excellence of his representation.

Those who have undertaken the duty of *tabligh* have a lot to learn from the behavior and conduct of the noble Prophet. The only condition of conquering the hearts and souls of others is to practice and live everything that is preached, just like the Prophet did.

For example, if a person wishes to explain the beauty of *Tahajjud* to others, he must first get up in the middle of the night and offer it by weeping until his Prayer mat is soaked with his tears. Otherwise, he will be slapped with the following verse, *"O you who believe! Why do you say what you do not do (as well as what you will not do)?"* (as-Saf 61:2) Hence he will never be effective.[60]

People Were Amazed by Abu Bakr's Representation

Companions who learned everything from the noble Prophet were also people of representation. In their lives, actions came before words. They would affect people with their role model lives.

Abu Bakr was one these individuals. At a time when Mecca did not allow believers to survive in its bosom, Abu Bakr was one of those people who were not given a chance in Mecca. Like those who had migrated to Ethiopia, he too thought of following his friends and migrating. On the road to Ethiopia, he ran into an idol-worshipper named Ibn'ud-Daghinna. He asked Abu Bakr: "Where are you going, O the son of Abu Kuhafa?"

Abu Bakr replied: "My community has banished me. They do not want to see me amongst them anymore."

[59] Ahmad ibn Hanbal, *Al-Musnad*, 2/231
[60] Gülen, M. Fethullah, *Sonsuz Nur-1*, İstanbul: Nil, 2007, pp. 262; 266

"How could they banish someone like you? You are a person who supports the poor, helps the widow and reaches out to the orphan. They cannot deprive someone like you from Mecca. Come with me, I will take you under my protection" replied, Ibn'ud-Daghinna.

They returned to Mecca and Ibn'ud-Daghinna announced that Abu Bakr was under his protection. However, this man was an idol-worshipper from Mecca, thus how long would he endure Abu Bakr, with his friends, behavior and the Qur'an? This remained to be seen.

Abu Bakr accepted the conditions put forward by this idol-worshipper and confined himself to his house. He continued reciting the Qur'an in his own house. After awhile, he built an extension to his house, a balcony-like structure located in front of his window and began to recite the Qur'an and offered his Prayers there.

Abu Bakr always had tears in his eyes, whenever he said "God", he could not hold his tears back and when he prayed, it was as if volcanoes were erupting in him. As he continued to pray and recite the Qur'an in a state of trance on his balcony, men, women and children would gather around his house and listen to him. The hearts of these people were gradually warming up to faith.

The leaders of the idol-worshippers were outraged by this as they spoke to Ibn'ud-Daghinna and said: "Release him from your protection or we will deal with him in a way that will damage your reputation as a protector. Do not let the people gossip behind your back."

Ibd-ud Daghinna asked Abu Bakr to stop reciting the Qur'an. He replied: "How could I refrain from the Qur'an? This is the Word of God. It was revealed so that it is announced to everyone. By God! Even if you take me out of your protection, I shall continue to do this under the protection of God!"

READING TEXT

How Does a White Man Serve an African?

We live in a poor suburb of Kenya. We have a simple life... A piece of dry bread we find is enough to make us happy for that day. My husband, children and I live in a small tin cabin. We never complain about our life. Many Kenyans live the way we do. We live in a narrow street and sewerage channels pass from the top of the dirt road that crosses our neighborhood. Death frequently visits our neighborhood. The scorching heat of the sun transforms our tin cabin into an oven. Malaria, dysentery and typhoid fever never leaves us alone.

There are also white men who live in our nation. We continue our lives without taking any notice of the space which exists between them and us. We have always been led to believe that white man is superior. They should be respected. Some people who come here to spread their religion always hinted that there is a difference between them and us. Although, they never mention it out in the open, they showed it with their actions and attitudes. They eat on different tables, they live in different houses and they ride on different vehicles.

We always dreamed of meeting white men who thinks like us. We hoped that the bad fortune of our Africa might change through such meeting. Yet, it never happened... Our story continued in this manner until the day we met these people. This was the day that my husband was employed by a Turkish school. Yes, these people were also white but their life-styles and manners had changed everything we believed about white people.

That summer, my husband Hasan started to work as a teacher in the Turkish school. I would never forget the words he uttered on the night of the day he had commenced his employment there: "Some of the administrative staff and teachers are white but these people are different to all the white men we know. We work under same conditions, we share the same food and on the same table. You may not believe this but they treat me and other Kenyans just as the way they treat their white friends. A white man brought us tea and he served it to all of us with a tray. The principal called me to his room and collected information about the living conditions in our neighborhood."

The things my husband explained were fascinating to me. How could a white man serve the Africans and share his food on the same table? These were behaviors that we had never seen before. I said to Hasan: "Maybe they are not sincere. They are new here and perhaps they need our support. A few months later they will begin to act like the other white people." However, months had gone by and their manners did not change, on the contrary, with each passing day, they came closer to us.

Each night when my husband came home, he would talk about them. I was looking for an opportunity to meet these people. I always carried a doubt in my head, as I thought to myself: "White man will never see himself as equal to us." The behavior of these people could be the policy of the school. One evening, Hasan came home and with excitement in his eyes, he said: "Fatima, here is your chance to meet them. The principal wants to visit our home with a few guests from Turkey."

I was surprised because I thought such thing was not possible. Moreover, I was a bit upset with Hasan as I thought he was joking with me. I said to him: "Stop joking around with me." Hasan replied: "I am not joking, they are coming tomorrow evening."

My husband seemed quite serious. I knew him very well hence his tone of voice and facial expression indicated that he was not joking. I was a bit confused and this was evident on my face. I replied with a stern voice: "White men will never come to our house!" Suddenly, I began to weep. Why was I crying? Did these tears which I was shedding symbolize the Africa that I longed for so many years? Were these the light-faced people that we were waiting for? I could not wait for the next day. I had reservations: "Would they really come to our home?" What would they think of the conditions in which we live?

Then they came and one by one they hugged my husband. Then they greeted me with respect and kindly asked how I was. I was nervous as I felt like weeping with joy. These white men had greeted me like no one before with pure sincerity and genuineness. This was the first time I had seen an African and a white men hug each other with so much honesty. More importantly, they took my children into their arms, stroked their heads and kissed them. They looked quite happy in our tin cabin and showed no sign of discomfort. They had brought gifts to all of us. They sat with us for hours comfortably and with no hesitation.

This was the moment that I realized these people were the people with faces of light which we had been waiting for. Our tin cabin was witnessing a historical event. I believed that these were the people who would change the dark fate of our Africa.[61]

Let Your Manners Speak and Your Tongue Be Silent

In Islam action and manners are essential principles. The two elements that affect people the most is behavior and attitude. In conveying the truth and righteousness to people, the main tool for Muslims should be their manners rather than their words. Behind the guidance of people who run to faith, there is a thing which is more effective than mere words and this is the representation of Islam through its spiritual life. When the disciples of Prophet Isa, peace be upon him, and the Companions of Prophet Muhammad, peace and blessings be upon him, interacted with people of different nations and explained the truths to them, they did not know their language and they were strangers to their customs. However, they entered the hearts of these people with their manners and good conduct.

This means that a Muslim's behavior should come before his speech. His actions should confirm his speech so that he is not dubbed as a liar by the side of God and he does not lose his reputation amongst the people. In our religion, being seen as a righteous person is not an important thing but being a righteous person is important. In His Qur'an, God Almighty says: *"Pursue, then, what is exactly right (in every matter of the Religion), as you are commanded (by God), and those who, along with you, have turned (to God with faith, repenting their former ways, let them do likewise); and do not rebel against the bounds of the Straight Path (O believers)! He indeed sees well all that you do"* (Hud 11:112). The verse does not only say: "Be truthful in your words and try to convince others with your truth." It says: "So remain on a right course as you have been commanded" with your actions and behavior.

Indeed, in our religion, presentation is not important, "being" is important; preaching and advocating is not important but living and

---

[61] *Zaman Ailem Dergisi*, issue 116, pp. 17–20

role modeling is important. For this reason, being effective in preaching depends on representation. So words can only have an impact if they are reflected onto behavior and also if they are spoken with an intention to earn the pleasure of God.

READING TEXT
Universal Language: The Language of Conduct

Travelling to other nations in order to spread the Divine message provides an important opportunity to learn new languages. Every Prophet conveyed his message through the tongue of his people. However, the success of the disciples cannot be based solely on the fact that they learned the language of the people who they invited to religion. I like to base this argument on a very significant historical event. Indeed, disciples have been quite effective in their *tabligh* in foreign lands. Their success lies in a universal language which they spoke. This language was the language of conduct and good manners. From the noble Messenger of God to his Companions and from the Companions to this day, the sultans of hearts have conquered many hearts and souls using this very language.

How the Companions learn the language of the people so rapidly in foreign lands is not that important. It might be that God rewarded them with this ability in return for their enthusiasm to spread the message of Islam or perhaps it was the fruits of their dedication.

For example, a Companion of the Prophet would leave Medina and travel to Spain for a higher purpose. He did not know their language or culture. The only thing that kept him on his feet was his dedication to this great cause and the dynamics which continuously nourished him. Not knowing the language was a disadvantage but it was a situation where causes had stopped and the Divine help had arrived. In recognition of his weakness, he lived the truth and conveyed his message through actions and good conduct. As a result, many people in the region came running towards the warm atmosphere of faith which he had formed.

When Mus'ab ibn Umayr left for Medina, he knew 12 verses from the Qur'an. Perhaps, the words he had spoken in Medina did not exceed five-hundred yet he was speaking with such a delicate language of manners that even the most stone-hearted people melted in his presence. Within a year, he came to Aqaba with seventy-two people.

It is also possible to show thousands of such examples in this day and age. For example, I like to share a story explained to me by some friends who enrolled in a language course following the September 11 tragedy. Muslims were treated differently after this tragic incident. It was a time when the media was portraying Muslims as people to be feared and this was the time that these friends had enrolled in the English classes. Because of their religion others were looking at them with spying eyes. Although they felt uncomfortable from these suspicious glances, they showed patience in the name of God and tried to explain themselves with their manners and behavior. The Holy Qur'an explains: *"Every one acts according to his own character..."* (al-Isra 17:84). This means that everyone shows their character through their manner. As these particular friends displayed their characters through their manners, everyone got their share out of the atmosphere they had formed. They had earned the appraisal of everyone through the way they sat, walked, ate, spoke, behaved and displayed their gentleness. On the second day of the course, people apologized to them for the inappropriate behavior displayed by some students hence the good manners of these friends were appreciated.

Another incident they had experienced was: A foreign student who was in the same class stressed that he hated and despised Turks. As a reason he used an example from his country of origin, arguing that he had witnessed some incidents in which Turks had behaved in an unacceptable manner. They explained to him that these people do not represent the entire Turkish nation and that in every nation one would find good and evil people. A short while after, these friends purchased some imported foods from Turkey and shared them in the class. Gradually, they became the centre of attention during the recess. Soon, the entire class began to develop a feeling of affection for these people.

One day, a student in the class invited them to a dinner in his house. Following the dinner, they offered their Prayers and interact with each other in a friendly atmosphere. As they left the house, their hosts made the following commentary: "Now we have four Turkish-Muslim brothers."

The tremors of September 11 and the negative approaches of the media had formed an unbearable atmosphere for the Muslims. However, these friends who had received a warm response from their classmates were encouraged from the positive developments. Their enthusiasm and eagerness had increased thus they evaluated the situation with the following remarks: "If every Muslim carried the attributes which they should possess, and applied them in their daily lives, there would be no obstacles they could not overcome in the name of these exalted ideals."

Let us conclude our topic with the words of a hero of role modeling: "If we could implement the values of faith in our lives within their real essence, then the followers of other religions will embrace this religion in masses." The existence of ideals and thoughts depends on its representatives. If the Companions of the noble Prophet had not lived the Qur'an as it should be lived, the Qur'an would have become a tongue-tied orphan. Looking at the issue from this perspective, if we do not want our values to turn into an orphan, then we need to take extreme care with our representation. Otherwise, we would pay dearly for our negligence. Therefore, one should not say: "How can I be a role model when I do not have much knowledge?" One should say: "It is more important to know a little but practice it through representation than to know a lot." Following this principle will provide a guarantee for us and the future generations.[62]

If You Are Saying It, Then Do It

A person's value by the side of God and his effectiveness in public is proportional to his abstinence from what is prohibited by God and fulfillment of the religious obligations. Words and actions are the two

---

[62] Gülen, M. Fethullah, "Hal Dili," http://tr.fgulen.com/content/view/10690/18/

important languages of explaining and spreading the truths of faith. This sole language which appears to be two-sided can produce amazing results if it is correctly implemented. The marks left by those who do not fall into contradiction with their words and actions will be lasting.

A person who sleeps through the night with lassitude should be ashamed to talk about the *Tahajjud* (the Night) Prayer. If he is not offering his Prayers in serenity and tranquility, then he should refrain from defining a perfect Prayer. The effectiveness of the topics that relate to God depends on the practices of the individual who explains them.

However, the verse, *"O you who believe! Why do you say what you do not do (as well as what you will not do)? Most odious it is in the sight of God that you say what you do not (and will not) do,"* (as-Saf 61:2–3) should not be misunderstood. When the verse asks "why", it is not implying that you should not say what you do not do. What it is actually saying is: "Since you are saying it then you should be doing it." So, saying something and not doing it draws the punishment of God. This means that the verse is not suggesting that one shouldn't say the things he does not do himself, but it is indicating that one should be determined to practice what he preaches.

Some Companions who had similar concerns about the issue asked the noble Prophet. Anas ibn Malik explains: "We asked the Prophet of God: "O Messenger of God, should we not encourage people to do good and prevent them from doing evil, if we are not practicing everything perfectly?" The noble Prophet replied: "No! Even if you do not practice everything perfectly, you should still invite others to good and if you are not able to protect yourselves from all the unlawful things, you should still prevent others from doing evil.[63]

Conveying the message and practicing the religious obligations are two different forms of worship. If you abandon both, you are committing two sins, but if you abandon one, you are committing one sin hence you are confining yourself to ineffectiveness. Saying what

---

[63] Al-Ghazali, *Ihya*, 2/329

you do not do or not practicing what you are saying will draw the Divine punishment and it will break the power of effectiveness. Furthermore, it will have a negative impact on your credibility and your words will have no effect thus they will be forgotten very quickly.[64]

People Should Say "There Is No Lie on This Face"

In this day and age some people, who are hungry for our religion, stay away from it because of the un-Islamic attitudes and behaviors of some Muslims. There are many examples of this. Here is one example:

During Ramadan, the people of a village in Erzurum organized a sermon to be delivered by İbrahim Hakkı, a renowned scholar of the era. They paid money to a non-Muslim individual who worked as a servant to pick the Imam with his horse and bring him to the village. The non-Muslim servant arrived to the house of the Imam but there was only one horse. So the Imam decided to take turns in riding the horse, just as Umar did when he travelled to Jerusalem with his servant. The servant tried to refuse the offer arguing that the villagers would be upset with him but the Imam insisted: "Son, we do not know what will happen to us at the time of our last breath. You are worried about the admonishment of the villagers yet I am worried about the Judgment Day when I shall stand before God and answer for my life on earth." The imam would not take no for answer, he had already made his mind up.

As Divine wisdom decided, when they were about to enter the village, just like in the case of Umar, it was the servant's turn to ride the horse. The servant was afraid of the villagers so he decided to give up on his right to mount the horse. He requested that İbrahim Hakkı remained on the horse as they entered the village. However, the Imam insisted: "It is your turn to ride the horse!"

He entered the village walking in front of the horse. As the villagers saw this, they gathered around the servant and began to scream at him: "How could you be so disrespectful? Shame on you! You let

---

[64] Gülen, M. Fethullah, "Allahım, Bizi Kendimize Getir!", http://tr.fgulen.com/content/view/12100/9/

an old scholar walk when you ride the horse in your young age. Is this your loyalty? Did we ask you to do this?"

However, they stopped harassing the young man when İbrahim Hakkı explained the arrangement them made between them. At that moment one of the villagers approached the non-Muslim servant and said: "You have seen the level of virtue here. Why don't you become a Muslims?"

After a few moments of consideration, the servant made the following noteworthy statement: "If you are inviting me to your religion, I will never accept! But if you are talking about the religion of this old man, I have already embraced it during our journey."

Yes, a person of *tabligh* should be so sensitive that for the sake of God, the Prophet, his religion and his people, he should let others claim: "There is no lie on this face." People who look at him should reach the following conclusion: "If it is his religion that gives him such perfect manners and a dignified character then there could be no lie in this religion either."

The Eminence of Bediüzzaman's Representation

Bediüzzaman, a radiant scholar who has lived every minute of his burdensome life serving the Qur'an and the reality of faith, has conveyed the truths of faith and represented them throughout his life.

After fleeing from captivity in Russia, Bediüzzaman came to İstanbul. An interesting incident occurred during his stay in İstanbul. It was the time of the traditional Kağıthane festival when Bediüzzaman and his three friends, Molla Seyid, Taha and Hacı İlyas, who were members of parliament, got on a small boat. Both sides of Haliç, from the Galata Bridge to Kağıthane were crowded by Greek, Armenian and other women from İstanbul. As they travelled with the boat, they were passing by these women who were celebrating the festival. In his own words, Bediüzzaman was not even aware of this. Molla Taha and Hacı İlyas were checking him out to see if he would look around. After travelling for an hour, they said: "We are amazed at you. You did not even take a glance."

Bediüzzaman replied: "I do not wish for such things because they are unnecessary, transient, sinful pleasures which result in suffering and sorrow."

Bediüzzaman stayed in İstanbul for a total of ten years which consisted of three separate visits. In his own words, he had never glanced at a *haram* once.

When he travelled to Van from Ankara in order to support the National Resistance, a man named Molla Hamid (Ekinci) was at his service. One day, Bediüzzaman said to him: "Just as a small fire could spread to the entire forest and burn it down, so too, looking at *haram* will gradually eat away all the good deeds of a believer. I fear the consequences of such man would be gruesome."

Bediüzzaman was showing great effort and exertion to explain the truths to people through such a high caliber of representation. The biggest impact he made on people was through his tongue of conduct, his manners and representation.

A Man of Representation: Tahiri Ağabey

Bediüzzaman lived a life of self-sacrifice with the utmost determination, a mind-boggling zeal and attitude without making any concessions. Like him, those who studied by his side also became great role models for people around them. From Hulusi Efendi to Hodja Sabri Efendi, from Hafız Ali to Hasan Feyzi Efendi and from Rüşdü Çakın to Mustafa Sungur, all of these giants of righteousness represented the truths to the best of their abilities. On this noble path, they were loyal and faithful. They were the genuine role models of fidelity, faithfulness, representation, the spirit of *tabligh* and devotion.

According to Bediüzzaman's mentality, if there was a student of the *Risale-i Nur* in a certain region, this region was considered to be a conquered in the name of the faith and virtues. Bediüzzaman would consider all individuals who became his students as people who claim: "My support is for my people." The weight of explaining the faith and its truths could only be raised on the shoulders of valiant souls who had locked themselves onto great ideals.

Another brave soul who served Bediüzzaman on this noble path was Tahiri Mutlu. It was a period when the *Risale-i Nur* would be published for the first time and Bediüzzaman sent his students out to find about 100 liras for the printing costs. He had written *Ayatu'l Kubra* but they did not have the funds to publish it.

When Tahiri Mutlu heard this, he said: "Master, give me three days." Then he ran to the village centre and announced that everything he possessed was up for sale. This wealth included a rose garden which he had inherited from his grandfather.

A relative who heard this came to him and said: "Tahiri! What are you doing? How will you survive?" He replied: "Why are you worried about my situation? I want to sell the garden, if you are interested then purchase it, if not I will sell it to someone else." His relative gave him the money and purchased the garden with tears pouring out of his eyes. Tahiri Ağabey brought the money to Bediüzzaman and *Ayatu'l Kubra* was printed with the sacrifice he made.

The devoted generations of today should not fall back in this blessed race hence they should use their freewill in its own rights to keep up with these unique individuals. When any of these individuals travelled to a certain region, a storm erupted there and changes in the name of faith and God began to take place. For this reason, it is important to act in accordance with consistency and by fulfilling the requirements of the freewill. If we show the necessary dedication and effort, God will make this job a part of our nature. In turn, we will stand firmly and upright on our ground without any discouragement and disheartenment.

READING TEXT
Since Your Faith Is So Beautiful,
I Shall Too Embrace Islam!

Abu Hanifa's neighbor was concerned because he had not seen him for a few days. He was not a Muslim but he respected and loved this unique scholar. He had never witnessed a bad treatment from him. Moreover, Abu Hanifa was there, whenever he needed something.

The neighbor learned that Abu Hanifa was ill and decided to visit him. He greeted him as he walked in through the door. There was a bad odor in the room but he did not mention it as he smiled and said: "May God restore your health neighbor."

Abu Hanifa replied: "Thank you brother, may God be pleased with you."

The smell in the room had not gone away. He could not hide his curiosity any longer as he wondered where the smell was coming from. He knew that Muslims were extremely careful with their hygiene so there had to be another reason for this bad odor. Before he asked, he saw a wall which was covered with a sheet. Then he asked: "Can you smell the odor too?"

The great Imam refrained from replying but he realized that he was waiting for an answer as he stared right into his eyes. Reluctantly, the Imam nodded his head indicating that he could smell it too. The neighbor who wanted to find out the source of the awful smell lifted the sheet which covered the wall. Abu Hanifa had no other option but to explain: "Dear neighbor, the dirty water coming from your house is leaking through my wall. This is the source of the unpleasant smell."

The man was shocked as he asked: "Why didn't you tell me this before?"

"How could I complain to you just like that? What about the rights that neighbors have over one another, for God's sake?"

The non-Muslim neighbor thought about how Islam gives great value to human beings. Then he said: "It is Islam that gives you this beauty."

Abu Hanifa replied: "The beauty belongs to Islam."

"Since your faith is so beautiful, I shall become a Muslim too," replied the neighbor.

The neighbor declared the testimony of faith and embraced Islam. A simple kindness was enough to guide him onto the right path. Imam Abu Hanifa's representation of his religion had caused another human being to embrace Islam.

QUESTIONS

1. Who is the Companion who said: "O Messenger of God, as the kings of the world sleep in their bird-feathered beds now, you sleep on a mat made up of straws. It has made marks on your body. You are the Messenger of God and you deserve a comfortable life more than anyone else!"

    a. Abu Bakr

    b. Umar ibn Khattab

    c. Usman ibn Affan

    d. Ali ibn Abi Talib

2. From the perspective of representation and tongue of conduct, what should a person who is explaining the virtues of *Tahajjud* do?

    a. Possess a good knowledge about the topic

    b. Conduct a comprehensive research on the topic

    c. First the person must perform *Tahajjud* himself and soak his Prayer mat with his tears.

    d. The social and psychological aspects of the topic must be researched.

3. Who is the *Risale Nur* student who sold his property in order to publish the *Ayatu'l Kubra*?

    a. Tahiri Mutlu Ağabey

    b. Hulusi Ağabey

    c. Hafız Ali Ağabey

    d. Hasan Feyzi Ağabey

4. Which of the below statement is incorrect?

    a. In taking the message of faith and religion to others one should use the tongue of conduct more than his words.

    b. A believer's behavior should always precede his words, thus his attitude and conduct should guide his words.

    c. In our religion preaching is more important than practicing.

    d. In our religion, appearing to be righteous is not important, but being righteous is important.

5. Who is the Jewish scholar who embraced Islam when he saw
   the Prophet and said: "There is no lie on this face. Only a
   Messenger of God can possess such a face."
   a. Abdullah ibn Salam
   b. Ibn'ud-Daghinna
   c. Abdullah ibn Masud
   d. Abdullah ibn Abbas

4

UKHUWAH: BROTHERHOOD

I request of my brothers that they are not offended at one another
due to discomfort, or distress of the spirit, or fastidiousness, or
being deceived by Satan's wiles, or at the offensive language uttered
by some of them. They should not say that their honor has been
insulted. I take on myself any bad words that are uttered. They
should not be offended. If I had a hundred honors, I would sacrifice
all of them for love and cordiality among my brothers.[65]

What Does *Ukhuwah* Mean?

The term *ukhuwah* comes from the Arabic root word *akh*,
which means brother, therefore *ukhuwah* means brotherhood.
When the term brotherhood is mentioned, the first thing
that comes to mind is siblings born from the same parents. However,
in our religion there is also a brotherhood (or sisterhood) which comes
from belief in the same faith. Our Lord explains this in the Holy
Qur'an: *"The believers are but brothers, so make peace between your brothers; and keep from disobedience to God in reverence for Him and piety..."*
(al-Hujurat 49:10).

This verse declares all believers as brothers and sisters no matter
what part of the world they are from. All believers who have faith in
God, His noble Messenger and the Holy Qur'an and turn to the same
kiblah and pray are brothers. Believers are each others' friends, Companions and soul mates. Islam considers brotherhood in faith as higher
than biological kinship and racial relationship and hence gives it more
significance. In a general sense this is called brotherhood in religion.

---

[65] Nursi, Said, *The Flashes*, İstanbul: Sözler, 2000, p. 359

Such brotherhood establishes a bond between all believers through the essentials of faith and piety. The following verse explains this explicitly:

> And hold fast all together to the rope of God, and never be divided. Remember God's favor upon you: you were once enemies, and He reconciled your hearts so that through His favor, you became like brothers. You stood on the brink of a pit of fire, and He delivered you from it. Thus, God makes His signs of truth clear to you that you may be guided (to the Straight Path in all matters, and be steadfast on it.) (Al Imran 3:103)

In the above verse, the Almighty God reminds us of the two tribes of Aws and Hazraj who were illustrious archenemies during the era of ignorance and how they became brothers through Islam. According to historical records these two tribes were at war with each other for 120 years and became brothers after accepting Islam.

The brotherhood encouraged by the Holy Qur'an necessitates love and respect, trust and compassion, mutual support and sharing of joy and sorrow. One of the factors that help believers attain the gratification of faith is: loving each other for the sake of God. Those who love each other for the sake of God will benefit from the shade of the Divine Throne on the Day of Judgment where no shades could be found. Those who love each other for God; come together and console one another; visit each other for God; converse and help each other are those who deserve the love of God.[66]

Our noble Prophet advises us to come together and to refrain from disunity. He informs us that God's aid is with the *jamaat* (congregation) and there is *rahmah* (compassion) in unity and *azhab* (punishment) in disunity.[67]

What Brotherhood Requires

There are very important responsibilities and rights in the brotherhood of faith. Believers are genuine brothers (sisters) and they are each oth-

---

[66] *Sahih al-Bukhari*, Iman, 9, 14, Adab, 42; *Sahih Muslim*, Iman, 67, Birr, 37, 38; *Sunan at-Tirmidhi*, Iman, 10; Ahmad ibn Hanbal, *Al-Musnad*, 5/233, 247

[67] *Sunan at-Tirmidhi*, Fitan, 7

er's eyes and guides. They do not betray, tyrannize and deceive each other. They do not look upon each other's wealth, chastity or life with evil eyes. On the contrary, they consider these as their own values and protect them accordingly.

Brotherhood in faith is an important factor that eliminates the small conflicts which may exist between the believers. A believer's hatred for another believer is a sign of hypocrisy. A believer cannot be in a not-speaking terms with another believer. If a believer does not wish for his brother what he wishes for himself; if he is jealous and spiteful of his brother and if he holds a certain enmity towards his brother, this is an indication that he does not possess true faith.

In a *hadith*, our noble Prophet describes the necessary bond between believers: "The bond between believers is like the bond between the components which keep the building together"[68] A situation where the opposite occurs, believers will lose the power of *jamaat*, they will slacken and weaken and as a result there will be no one left to establish the good and abolish the evil on earth. This in turn will cause the surfacing of great mischief on earth.[69]

When Jafar ibn Abi Talib was martyred at the Battle of Muta, our noble Prophet wept a lot and felt great sorrow, but displayed great patience as he uttered the following words: "A believer cares about his brother."[70]

Our noble Prophet cared about everyone and felt sorrow for their sorrow. When the news of Jafar ibn Abi Talib's martyrdom came, the noble Prophet explained the reason for his sadness but at the same time he was teaching his Companions and his followers in general about the required sensitivity that an ideal believer should possess.

In following the noble Prophet and being his friend, we should take into consideration how his Companions cared about each other. On earth, Islam was lived in the best way possible by the Companions of the noble Prophet. The dynamics which made them Compan-

[68] *Sahih al-Bukhari*, Salah, 88, Mezalim, 5; *Sahih Muslim*, Birr, 65; *Sunan at-Tirmidhi*, Birr, 18; *Sunan an-Nasa'i*, Zakah, 67
[69] Ünal, Ali, "Cemaat", *Sosyal Bilimler Ansiklopedisi*, 3/25
[70] Ibn Hamza, *Asbabu Wurudi'l-Hadis*, 3/252

ions of the Prophet were concealed in the title which was given to them. These people who befriended each other; who displayed brotherhood in its purest form; who abandoned unruliness to believe in the magical power of obedience, showed great care for each other as they made history.

In human history, one could not find another community who loved and bonded with each other through the brotherhood of faith to produce a legendary love, like the Companions of the noble Prophet. The gallantry of these people who gave water to their brothers even in the moment of death and people who gave half of everything they possessed to their refugee brothers, who had migrated for their religion, cannot be explained in many volumes of books.

Our noble Prophet explains the requirements of brotherhood in the following *hadith*: "Muslims are brothers. When a Muslim meets another Muslim, he responds to his brother's greeting with similar words or in a more beautiful way; he gives advice to him when he requests it; he supports him against his enemies when he asks for help; he shows him the right path when he asks for it; if he requests a loan to be used against his enemies, he gives it to him, providing that it is not used against another Muslim; he would even give his brother the paradise, if he requests it as a loan."[71]

Using the verses and *hadith*s as the main source, Imam al-Ghazali lists the principles of brotherhood and the rights that should be protected between brothers, friends and mates:

1. Brothers need to support each other financially and run to each other's aid voluntarily.
2. Brothers can also request physical help from each other.
3. Brothers defend one another during the absence of the other and conceal each other's mistakes and faults.
4. Brothers do not see each other's faults hence they forgive them.
5. Brothers remember each other with compassion and mercy during life and death.
6. Brothers treat each other with loyalty and sincerity.

---

[71] Ali al-Muttaki, *Kanzu'l-Ummal*, 1/151–152

7. Brothers do not approach each other with a cold attitude thus they refrain from actions that may trouble each other. They know that inconveniences should be tolerated in the name of good relations.[72]

READING TEXT

Believers Are Like the Organs of the Same Body

One day the organs of a body called a meeting amongst themselves. They were all complaining about working for the stomach. The stomach appeared to be doing nothing much and without a rest it could not do a thing anyway. All the organs seemed quite upset. At the conclusion of the meeting, all the organs decided that they would not fulfill all the requests of the stomach anymore. They were not going to spend all their efforts on the stomach.

The eyes were saying that they would not choose anymore; hands stressed that they would not hold and mouth declared that it would not eat anymore. The teeth decided not to chew and the feet claimed that they would not walk for the stomach anymore.

They did what they claimed and left the stomach without food. However, before long, the eyes began to blur, hands began to shake, mouth dried up, teeth began to decay and feet had no energy even to take a step. It was obvious that although the stomach could not survive without them, in order to survive they also needed the stomach.

They realized all the organs of the body were supporting each other and it was impossible to sustain life without such harmony and unity. This meant that everyone was working for each other and the absence of one organ would be felt by all the others.[73]

In the words of our Prophet, the situation of believers in relation to each other is the same as the relation between the organs and the cells of the body.[74] Just as when there is a pain in one part of the body, the entire body feels it and thus makes an attempt to get rid of

[72] Al-Ghazali, *Ihya*, 2/170
[73] Akar, Mehmet, *Mesel Ufku*, İstanbul: Timaş, 2008, p. 128
[74] *Sahih al-Bukhari*, Adab, 27; *Sahih Muslim*, Birr, 66

it, all Muslims should also feel the pain felt by their brother and accordingly they should act with responsibility and look for ways to solve the problem. An evil done to a Muslim activates all Muslims hence they help each other in all kinds of situations.

What Are the Viruses That Threaten the Essence of Brotherhood?

Our noble Prophet talks about the viruses that threaten the bonds of brotherhood which hold Muslims together: "O servants of God do not give space to wrongful assumptions, because they are the biggest of lies. Do not look for faults; do not chase news; do not compete with each other; do not be jealous of each other; do not curse each other and do not turn your back on each other. Be brothers in the way God has commanded. Believers are brothers. Believers do not tyrannize or insult each other and they do not deprive each other. For a person, insulting his brother is enough of an evil. The blood, wealth and dignity of a Muslim are *haram* for all the other Muslims. God does not look upon your appearance, but He looks at your hearts and deeds." The noble Prophet pointed to his heart and said: "Be cautious! Piety is here! Do not make a sale above each other's sale. O the servants of God, establish brotherhood amongst you. It is not *halal* for a Muslim to abstain from speaking to his brother for more than three days."[75]

This *hadith* focuses on factors that harm brotherhood. Let us address them one by one: When we investigate the causes of big conflicts, we see that false assumptions and misinterpretations play a great role in them. This is called *suizan* (false assumption). *Hüsnüzan* (good assumption) is always profitable. If it turns out to be correct then you have hit the target. If it turns out to be incorrect, you have not lost anything. On the contrary, you have not committed the sin of backbiting and perhaps you have prevented a big conflict.

Another thing that disturbs people a lot is the act of looking for people's mistakes or faults or investigating their private issues. Eaves-

---

[75] *Sahih al-Bukhari*, Nikah, 45, Adab 57, Faraid 2; *Sahih Muslim*, Birr, 28; *Sunan Abu Dawud*, Adab, 40

dropping on others to learn about their private lives is a terrible disease. Along with being an act of bad manners, it can also damage the relationships between individuals.

Listening to private conversations is also a violation of human rights. Whether it is done on an individual level or on an international level, spying on others and recording their private affairs, is an ugly act and a harmful disease. Following the world wars, international espionage has increased significantly and it has become a serious threat to world peace.

Competition: if it is done in a race for good and virtue and without destruction, then the Holy Qur'an encourages it.[76] However, if it is done with certain immoral behavior, then it reminds us of the sins which are committed with the excuse of competition.

Jealousy and envy is a passionate desire for something that someone else possesses and wishing that you had it instead of the other person. In other words, it means feeling uncomfortable about the qualities and virtues (blessed by God) to someone else. Consequently, believers cannot be covetous. Just as fire eats away the wood, covetousness will eat away a person's good deeds and Divine rewards and it will kill his spirit.[77] Once again, in the words of our noble Prophet: "A heart cannot contain faith and jealousy at the same time."[78] A believer can only desire without malice. This means that if a believer sees a good merit on his brother and wishes that he could be like that too, it will be considered as envy without malice.

Another virus that threatens the solidity of brotherhood is using words that imply vanity and self-pride. Such behavior is quite dangerous for the person who has vanity and for the *jamaat* which he is a part of. Therefore, immodest person cannot throw his self-pride—which resembles an ice cube—into the pool of the *jamaat* so that it could melt, thus he could never become a person of service and one cannot think of such person surviving in a *jamaat* for too long.

---

[76] Al-Baqarah 2:148

[77] *Sunan Abu Dawud*, Adab 44; *Sunan ibn Majah*, Zuhd 22

[78] *Sunan an-Nasa'i*, Jihad, 8

READING TEXT

A philosopher was walking with his students just before sunset. One of his students asked: "Sir, the sun will set soon. When does light end and darkness begin?"

The philosopher pointed to some birds on a distant tree and asked: "What type of birds are they?"

The students replied: "They are fieldfares."

A few minutes later it was getting dark and he asked again: "What type of a tree is that?"

The students were under a bit of strain as they replied: "That is an oak."

A few minutes later it got a bit darker and he asked once again: "See those animals over there; what are they?"

This time the students were giving different answers: "Sheep... cattle... dogs."

The philosopher said: "One day when you are walking on the street and you run into someone. If you are able to say: "This is my brother (sister)" even though you could not see his face or the type of clothes he is wearing, this is the day that darkness has ended and light has come.

Believers Must Love Each Other

You ask why? It is because God and His Messenger command it. Some of our brothers (sisters) may have unpleasant characters or we may not like their attitude. This does not mean we should turn our backs to them. We need to support and in some way embrace them.

Our noble Prophet commands us: "O servants of God! Establish brotherhood amongst you." Yes, this is an order and the person who is giving it, is not some ordinary man. He is the Messenger of God who was given a mission. In this day and age, some wrongful acts ascribed to some Muslims within our nation and within other Muslim nations are affecting our judgment and perspective.

If there are mistakes made by Muslims and if we defend them only because they are Muslims, then we would be adding another mistake to their mistakes. Two wrongs do not make a right. On the other hand, claiming that these Muslims who make these mistakes cannot be considered as Muslims or uttering words that may harm Islam means falling into the traps set by people who work against Islam. Consequently, by concentrating on the negatives, we would be deprived from seeing the beauty of Islam.

Faith establishes a brotherhood which is more powerful than the one that originates from having the same father and mother. Even biological siblings may not trust each other sometimes, but brothers in faith trust each other in every aspect. They form an infinite circle of trust amongst each other. This reality is explained in the following verse: *"The believers are but brothers"* (al-Hujurat 49:10). A *hadith* mentioned above applies certain conditions to brotherhood:

Believers do not turn their backs to each other. They do not betray or tyrannize each other. They do not deprive or insult each other, because, for a human being, insulting his brother is enough of an evil.

Indeed, true faith is the insurance of life. Living beings are insured through faith. The reason for this is, the wealth, life and dignity of Muslims are *haram* to other Muslims hence they are under protection.

"Verily God does not look to your bodies nor to your faces but He looks to your hearts."[79] A person is defined by his actions. This means if a believer is carrying the attributes described above, then this is true faith. If on the other hand, believers are talking behind each other's backs, disliking each other, being jealous of each other, pointing to each other's faults, making wrongful assumptions, showing no tolerance for each other and if their deeds are formalities, if they do not come from the heart, it means true faith has not entered the hearts. It would be more appropriate to address such people with the following verse: *"O you who believe! Believe in God and His Messenger..."* (an-Nisa 4:136).

Our *hadith* concludes with the words: "Do not make a sale over your brother and do not refrain from speaking to each other for more than three days." This *hadith* is full of advice that would guide us in

---

[79] *Sahih Muslim*, Birr, 33; *Sunan ibn Majah*, Zuhd, 9

every part of our lives. It is like a road map for all believers in the world. Yes, these Prophetic advices are a road map for believers who have set the paradise as a goal for themselves. They show us the straight path, a path that has no deviations.

Abdullah ibn Umar explains: "The Messenger of God climbed the *minbar* and with a loud voice, he said: "O you people who have become Muslims with their tongues but whose hearts have not been blessed with faith yet! Do not torment the Muslims! Do not belittle them and do not investigate their private affairs, for whoever violates his brother's privacy, God will violate his privacy! And if God violates someone's privacy, no matter where he hides or what he conceals, God will bring it into open and will disgrace him!"

One day, Abdullah ibn Umar looked at the Ka'ba and said: "How glorious are you and your prominence! However, in reverence, a believer is higher and more venerable than you!"[80]

Let us conclude the topic with two *hadith*s from our noble Prophet: "Believers are brothers. They do not oppress each other and they do not leave each other alone in danger. Whoever takes care of his brother's need, God will take care of his need. Whoever solves his brother's problem, God will solve his problem on the Day of Judgment. Whoever conceals the shameful deed of his brother, God will conceal his shameful deeds on the Day of Judgment."[81]

"Whoever defends and protects the dignity and honor of his brother, God will turn his face away from hellfire on the Day of Judgment."[82]

READING TEXT

Such a Brotherhood!

Akif and Ali were genuine friends who loved each other more than biological brothers. They loved each other even more than their own lives. Everyone envied this friendship.

---

[80] *Sunan at-Tirmidhi*, Birr, 85
[81] *Sunan Abu Dawud*, Adab, 46; *Sunan at-Tirmidhi*, Hudud, 3; *Sahih al-Bukhari*, Mazalim, 3; Ikrah, 7; *Sahih Muslim*, Birr, 58
[82] *Sunan at-Tirmidhi*, Birr, 20

They had made an agreement between each other. Of course, this was a spiritual agreement. Akif called this agreement "righteousness." This meant that always encouraging the doing of good, refraining from telling your brother's faults to his face and doing this only for the sake of God. Moreover, it was helping your brother improve himself.

They believed that being righteous was the best solution for correcting mistakes and faults. A righteous person who reminds you of the truths and invites you to good deeds will help you maintain your path. With this intention, Akif said to his friend: "Brother, I wish to make an agreement with you."

"What kind of an agreement," asked Ali.

"I am giving you permission to warn me about all the bad things you see on me," replied Akif.

"I will accept this with a condition that you will do the same for me," said Ali.

"Ok then, it is done," replied Akif.

This was an agreement made between these two friends. Many years had gone by and nothing had changed between these genuine friends. However, a development which occurred that year had saddened both of them. Akif had to move to another city due to a new position. They consoled each other and promised they would visit each other frequently. This was a friendship that would last for eternity.

A month had gone by and Ali wanted to visit his friend Akif. He missed him so much. Every time he heard his name, he felt emotional. He did not want to delay this any longer. So he left for the city his friend lived in. On the way, he saw a strange man. He was sitting on the side of the road and seemed as if he wanted to say something to Ali. He walked towards the man and greeted him. Then Ali introduced himself to the man. This person was no ordinary man; he was an angel who had disguised himself as a human being. However, Ali was oblivious to this fact. The man asked: "Where are you going, son?"

"To visit a friend," replied Ali.

"Your friend must have done something exceptional for you and this is why you wish to repay him with your gratitude," the man said.

"No! I do not need to repay him. I love him for the sake of God and I wish to visit him for the love of God," said Ali.

"How wonderful! I will tell you a secret. I am an angel sent by God. Just as you love your brother for the sake of God, you should know that God also loves you a lot,"[83] he said.

Following the Great Migration, Our Noble Prophet Declared the Ansar and the Muhajirin as Brothers

When the noble Prophet migrated to Medina, many Muslims had also migrated before and after him. The Muslim population in Medina consisted of the Muhajirin who had migrated from Mecca and the Ansar who were the Muslims of Medina. Ansar were supporting the Muhajirin. From a religious perspective, the Ansar and the Muhajirin were already brothers, but our noble Prophet established a more personal brotherhood (*muakhat*) between the two groups, so that they could intermingle.

Abu Bakr was paired with Kharija ibn Zayd, Umar with Atban ibn Malik, Uthman with Aws ibn Sabit, Abu Ubayda with Sa'd ibn Muaz, Mus'ab ibn Umayr with Abu Ayyub al Ansari, Abdurrahman ibn Awf with Sa'd ibn Rabi and Salman Farisi with Abu Darda and they were all declared as brothers.[84]

This was a special kind of brotherhood. The objective was to encourage the Muslims of Medina to help the Muhajirin and at the same time get the two groups to intermingle. Whilst the Ansar supported the Muhajirin in a financial way, the Muhajirin were teaching them their religion. There were constant interactions between them. They would continuously visit each other and organize lectures and informal gatherings. They were walking together on the path to God (*sirat-al mustaqim*) as they supported and protected each other and shared the same faith and ideals. They had become genuine brothers, loyal Companions and friends who walked on the path of the righteous.

---

[83] *Sahih Muslim*, Birr, 38; Ahmad ibn Hanbal, *Al-Musnad*, 2/292

[84] *Sahih al-Bukhari*, Manaqibu'l-Ansar, 3, *Sahih Muslim*, Fadailu's-Sahaba, 203

The Ansar had opened their arms with sincerity and love, sharing everything they had with their brothers who had migrated from Mecca, leaving all their wealth behind for the sake of God. The two groups had formed a picture of brotherhood that would serve as an example for all future generations.

For example, Sa'd ibn Rabi whom the Prophet had matched up with Abdurrahman ibn Awf as brothers, brought all his wealth and said: "half of it is yours!" The answer given by the great Companion, Abdurrahman who was one of the ten people to be given the good news of paradise whilst on earth, was noteworthy: "May God bless your wealth. I do not need it. However, you can help me by showing me the way to the marketplace."[85]

The Almighty God describes this brotherhood in the Holy Qur'an: *"Remember God's favor upon you: you were once enemies, and He reconciled your hearts so that through His favor, you became like brothers"* (Al Imran 3:103). *"He has attuned their (the believers') hearts. If you had spent all that is on the earth, you could not have attuned their hearts, but God has attuned them"* (al-Anfal 8:63).

In the pages of history, one cannot find another example of such spiritual brotherhood and such a picture of nobility. Through such brotherhood different levels of society had interacted, the arrogance and enmity of tribalism were abolished and consequently an era which would serve as an example to all future centuries was lived. For this reason, the title given to this period was, "the Age of Happiness."

The inimitable portrayal of brotherhood displayed by the Ansar (the Helpers) towards the Muhajirin (the Emigrants) is celebrated by the Qur'an:

> Those who, before their coming, had their abode (in Medina), preparing it as a home for Islam and faith, love those who emigrate to them for God's sake, and in their hearts do not begrudge what they have been given; and (indeed) they prefer them over themselves, even though poverty be their own lot. (They, too, have a share in such gains of war.) Whoever is guarded against the ava-

---

[85] *Sahih al-Bukhari*, Manaqıbu'l-Ansar, 2

rice of his own soul—those are the ones who are truly prosperous. (al-Hashr 59:9)

Today's Muslims should take the Companions of the Prophet as an example and love each other only for the sake of God; they should not scorn or look down on each other; they should intermingle and interact; they should be tolerant towards each other and never neglect fidelity; they should distance themselves from backbiting; they should always be forgiving and wish for their faith brothers what they wish for themselves.

A special kind of brotherhood exists between two Muslim brothers will enhance the brotherhood in Islam in a general sense, for as long as this brotherhood does not harm other Muslims. Such brotherhood will establish strong bonds between the believers. However, if this brotherhood is established in a way that it neglects other Muslims or works against them, this would mean it has failed to achieve its objective. Such brotherhood has no religious merit. Since it would cause mischief and discrimination, thus it is detrimental and dangerous.

Examples of Brotherhood from the Age of Happiness

Our religion aims to establish societies which are based on fundamental unity, harmony and consistency. In the Qur'an, God Almighty informs us: *"So keep from disobedience to God in reverence for Him and piety, and set things right among yourselves to allow no discord; and obey God and His Messenger if you are true believers"* (al-Anfal 8:1).

Our noble Prophet also said: "I advise you to keep together and abstain from falling apart and scattering."[86] "The aid of God is with the *jamaat* (community). There is *rahmah* (compassion) in unity and there is *azab* (punishment) in disunity."[87]

The manners of the Age of Happiness consist of brotherhood, mutual support, munificence and *ithar* (thinking of your brother or sister before yourself). In connection to this, our noble Prophet showed extreme sensitivity towards stopping the growth of conflicts as he

---

[86] *Sunan at-Tirmidhi*, Fitan, 7

[87] *Ibid.*; Ahmed ibn Hanbal, *Al-Musnad*, 4/278, 375

moved quickly and swiftly to stop the disputes between Muslims before they got out of control. It is imperative that internal peace, mutual support and secure environment is established in a society so that good manners may bear its fruits and experienced widely.

Let us now take a look at how the noble Prophet handled certain disputes and disagreements: During the campaign of Banu Mustaliq, an argument erupted between two people who were carrying water from the well of Muraysi to the Ansar and the Muhajirin. When the man representing the Ansar called his friends to his aid and the man representing the Muhajirin called his friends to his aid, the dispute got out of control. The noble Prophet who heard about the quarrel came quickly to the scene and calmed everyone down. Fighting about such simple things was a custom of the era of ignorance. However, Islam had prohibited such conflicts as it encouraged people to live in harmony and peace. Muslims had a responsibility to live in peace and to support each other in the regions they resided. Muslims were brothers hence they lived accordingly.

Brothers in faith could not be allowed to enter into conflicts for no reason. For this reason, whenever there was a dispute somewhere, our noble Prophet would intervene immediately to resolve the issue between the parties involved.

Another example of the noble Prophet's efforts to stop a dispute amongst the Companions took place in Quba. The noble Prophet had exerted great effort during the dispute that had taken place in Quba. In order provide a quick solution to the issue he even delayed one of his precious Prayers which he would always offer on time. Here is the story of this particular incident:

One afternoon, an argument had erupted between the sons of Amr ibn Avf in Quba. The dispute had quickly turned into a fight. During the fight there were people throwing rocks at each other. Our noble Prophet who had heard about the fight rushed to Quba taking a few of his Companions along. Immediately, he took control of the situation and attempted to calm everyone down.

The time of the Prayer had entered and Bilal who was the *muezzin* of the Masjid an-Nabawi (the Prophet's Mosque) had called the *adhan*. The *jamaat* waited for awhile yet the Prophet had not returned from Quba. This meant the issue between the people of Quba had not been solved yet. The Messenger of God did not want to return until he established peace among the people. Delaying the Prayer was a good indication of this.

Meanwhile in Medina, Bilal said to Abu Bakr: "It seems like the noble Messenger is still busy with the peace process, perhaps you should lead the Prayer." Abu Bakr stood up and commenced to lead the Prayer. A few minutes after, the noble Messenger walked in and advanced towards the first row. Abu Bakr realized this and took a few steps back and the noble Messenger took his place at the *mihrab* and led the Prayer. [88]

This example teaches us that the noble Prophet was extremely sensitive about resolving disputes and the preservation of brotherhood between Muslims.

Why Did Abu Dharr Apologize to Bilal al-Habashi

Just as in all issues of life, we need to take extreme care with human relations and abstain from negative behavior and wrongful acts. Therefore, it is not good to make mistakes in human relations. However, insisting on a wrongful act is worse than the act itself. An appropriate behavior is abandoning a wrongful act as soon as it is noticed and making up for the mistake in the best possible way. The first step to take in this regard is to apologize and ask for forgiveness.

One day, for some reason, Abu Dharr belittled Bilal with the following words: "The son of a black woman!" The news quickly travelled to the noble Prophet. He then summoned Abu Dharr and said: "O Abu Dharr, are you insulting him because of his mother? This means the manners of the era of ignorance are still in you." Abu Dharr felt so ashamed that he placed his head at the door step of Bilal and said: "I will not get up from here unless Bilal steps on my face."

[88] Zebidi, Zeynü'd-din Ahmet, *Sahih-i Buhari Muhtasarı Tecrid-i Sarih Tercemesi ve Şerhi*, İstanbul: Diyanet Vakfı, 1984, 8, pp. 114–115

Although Bilal told him he had forgiven him already and there was no need for this, Abu Dharr insisted. Bilal had no other option hence with his feet he touched Abu Dharr's cheek."[89]

In the above incident, we see the repentance and sensitivity of a Companion who had caused a dispute. The most important point in this example is abstinence from insisting on a wrongful act. Not insisting on a wrongful act, repenting to God and asking for forgiveness from the people who have been wronged and turning towards righteousness are the qualities of a person of *taqwa* (piety).[90]

READING TEXT

The Brotherhood of Abu Bakr and Umar

Abu Darda explains an incident which he witnessed when he was with the noble Prophet:

One day when we sitting with the noble Messenger, Abu Bakr came running in with his garment rolled up all the way to his knees. He seemed quite panicky. The noble Messenger of God said: "Your friend must have squabbled with someone." Abu Bakr greeted the noble Prophet and then began to explain what had happen to him.

Apparently, there was a dispute between him and Umar ibn Khattab. However, Abu Bakr had overreacted and offended Umar. Although, he tried to apologize and asked for forgiveness, Umar was not interested. The noble Messenger asked for forgiveness from God on behalf of Abu Bakr and he repeated this for three times. Meanwhile, Umar also felt regretful about the whole incident hence went to Abu Bakr's house. When he couldn't find him there, he came to the gathering and walked in after greeting the Prophet.

Umar was about to explain what had happened but Abu Bakr noticed the change on the Prophet's face. He feared that Umar would be admonished and quickly intervened and said that it was his fault, as he sat on his knees. Abu Darda, who narrates the incident, says that

---

[89] *Ibid.*, 1, pp. 42–44
[90] See Al Imran 3:134–135

the Messenger of God addressed everyone and said that in the early days, when he commenced his mission of Prophethood, everyone he invited to Islam showed signs of hesitance, suspicion or denial, but Abu Bakr was the only person who believed his Prophethood without showing any hesitation. Then he said: "Now O my Companions! Will you leave my dear friend, who possesses such qualities and attributes, to me?"[91] Abu Darda concludes that following the Prophet's commendation, no one ever broke Abu Bakr's heart again.[92]

This is what brotherhood and Companionship is all about. The attitude of Abu Bakr and Umar within the framework of an argument is a beautiful example for the people of today who jump into arguments more than a few times a day.

Let us think about it and cross examine ourselves: how many times and with how many Muslims have we argued with? How many times have we overreacted and hurt the feelings of our friends? Moreover, how many times have we asked for forgiveness from God and apologized to our friends?

Or perhaps, our arguments have accumulated so much that we have broken our ties with our friends because we failed to act in the manner of Abu Bakr and Umar.

Are we behaving like hypocrites by refraining from the virtue of apologizing and acting as if nothing had happened? Why can't we offer our apology on time and with sincerity?

Would we not be left way behind the people of the era of contentment and from the manners of the Companions if we fail to adopt their virtuous behavior and manners?

All of us should make an effort to preserve our friendships, brotherhood and mutual love by behaving like Abu Bakr and Umar![93]

---

[91] *Sahih al-Bukhari*, Fadail al-Ashabi'n-Nabi, 5, 13; Zebidi, Zeynü'd-din Ahmet, Sahih-i Buhari Muhtasarı Tecrid-i Sarih Tercemesi ve Şerhi, İstanbul: Diyanet Vakfı, 1984, 9, p. 332

[92] *Ibid.*

[93] Algül, Hüseyin, *Bir Huzur İklimi Asr-ı Saadet*, İstanbul: Işık Yayınları, 2010, pp. 125–126

We Are Being Tested with Each Other

One should never forget that just as the Almighty God tests us with certain incidents and events, He also tests us with our friends and brothers. The Holy Qur'an states: *"And it is in this way that We try people through one another"* (al-Anfal 6:53). For this reason, we should look at our relationship with our brothers as being part of a Divine test hence we should consider all negative aspects of our relationship as threats to our friendship and as certain elements of the test.

If one does not accept that he is being tested from the very beginning, then he would assume that from the closest circle to disbelievers, everyone is against him, and that everyone is his enemy. Moreover, he would be in the assumption of "every branch I hold onto breaks off." On the other hand, if he realized that all of these things are part of the test, then such negative emotions and thoughts will gradually melt away.

We are human and thus we will make mistakes. This is quite normal. If you were to study human beings one by one and get them to talk to you through psychoanalyses, you would be surprised by what they will tell you about their friends. This is in human nature. This is why we need to be tolerant, benevolent and soft natured. As we have the ability to overcome mountains and cross rivers, we should also think of the faults of our friends as mountains to be conquered with the wings of gentleness and through patience, tolerance and kindness.

A person who requests an eternal happiness must first think of this: I am not wishing for something cheap. I am an aspirant of eternity. Remember what Bediüzzaman says: "O people, do you know where you are going, where you are being driven? You are going to the sphere of Mercy, to the peaceful Presence of the All-Beautiful One of Majesty. A happy life of 1,000 years in this world cannot be compared to an hour of life in Paradise, and 1,000 years of life in Paradise cannot be compared to an hour's vision of His Countenance of utmost beauty."[94]

---

[94] Nursi, Said, *The Letters*, New Jersey: The Light, 2007, p. 245

Our objective is extremely valuable and precious; accordingly, we need to tolerate and endure the hardship and difficult tests that come proportional to the magnitude of the purpose. There will be hills appearing in the form of displeasing words and unwanted behavior on the road to our grand objective. However, we should accept these from the beginning and for the sake of our magnificent purpose; we should consider them as components of the test and overcome them with good manners to continue our journey.

It is the duty of a believer to see the good side of his brothers rather than their bad sides and to appreciate their good sides by forgiving their mistakes, turning a blind eye to their faults and errors. For our religion has forbidden the act of looking for faults and encourages us to close our eyes when we see them unwillingly. Moreover, it considers forgiveness as charity (*sadaqa*).

In the Qur'an, our Lord describes such people with the following verse:

> They spend (out of what God has provided for them,) both in ease and hardship, ever-restraining their rage (even when provoked and able to retaliate), and pardoning people (their offenses). God loves (such) people who are devoted to doing good, aware that God is seeing them. (Al Imran 3:134)[95]

In one of his sermons, Fethullah Gülen explains the issue of being tested with each other:

"We are even tested with our brothers. This should be anticipated right from the beginning and it should be known that God will establish bridges of love between our hearts if we succeed in this test. Perhaps this test will conclude in our favor if we show patience, tolerance and lenience. And perhaps then the Almighty God will grant us what we want and establish a connection between our hearts. The second thing is: each individual must do what is necessary hence accept and appreciate one another. The third step is: the other brother must be informed of this acceptance and appreciation either directly or indi-

---

[95] Gülen, M. Fethullah, "Kardeşlik," Kırık Testi, 17 June 2002, http://tr.fgulen.com/content/view/12257/3/

rectly so that our actions are embraced by our hearts and our souls are convinced.

There is also a negative side to this relation and that is cautioning our brothers. Nevertheless, if they respect our views and opinion, then we should be able to tell their mistakes and errors to their face. However, this should be done with extreme care by refraining from haughtiness, self-importance, gestures and mimics that God is not pleased with. This means when we are explaining something to them we would be so careful so that their hearts do not retort to our views. If we are not able to speak directly then we should explain a related topic in public and let them take their share. However, we should never speak about the faults of others behind their backs. Even a gesture such as "O you mean that guy" about someone who is not present, is not an appropriate behavior for a believer. The Holy Qur'an considers even a gesture that intends to make fun of someone as backbiting: *"Waylun li-kulli humazatin lumazah."* Woe to every scorner and mocker! This means woe to people who make fun of others, mock them behind their backs and belittle them with facial gestures! Yes, even an act such as speaking about a person jacket and saying that it is too short or too big, is considered as backbiting. A *hadith* regards backbiting as a major sin as it resembles it to committing adultery with a close relative. Could someone be this shallow? On the one hand, you are going to call him a brother and on the other, you are going to talk behind his back using an insignificant excuse to justify yourself. When your brother hears that you have been talking about him with great admiration and love, he would feel much closer to you; however, if he hears that you have been backbiting, he will do the opposite and distance himself from you. Perhaps, he will feel resentment and enmity after hearing about all the displeasing words and behavior. Even if you tried to make up for it by uttering a few nice words, he will be suspicious as he will wonder, "Why is he being nice to me now."

A person must lock his tongue from the beginning and refrain from talking behind his brothers. Gossip and backbiting are terrible things. One must abstain from things for which he would need to apologize later. However, if he had made this mistake and committed a sin against his brother by talking behind his back, gossiping or backbiting, he should then cleanse himself immediately by repeating everything he said to his brother's face and with remorse and regret he should ask for forgiveness by assuring his brother that such a thing will never happen again. Moreover, he should never repeat this kind of behavior again. Sometimes when you say to someone, "I have spoken these words behind your back", it may leave a mark in his heart. In order to avoid this, one must zip his mouth right from the beginning and abstain from backbiting at all times.[96]

How Did Bediüzzaman Explain Brotherhood?

In his works, Bediüzzaman mentions brotherhood and unity of Muslim brothers as the second most important topic after faith. He focuses on the unity of Islam and brotherhood of religion with persistence and considers this as a result of Muslims' connection to God with faith without pretense. He shows his sensitivity on the issue with the following words: "… there is no hypocrisy in performing the obligatory acts of religion. The obligatory act of greatest importance at the present time is Islamic unity."[97] In the same chapter, he says: "The way of this Union is love; its enmity is only for ignorance, poverty, and strife."[98] With this statement, Bediüzzaman declares that unity and brotherhood can only be formed through love. The reason for this is, faith necessitates love and Islam necessitates brotherhood.

Bediüzzaman compares the brotherhood in Islam with national and personal brotherhood and concludes that the first is loyal and genuine hence it encompasses the entire *ummah* of Islam; the latter, on the other hand, is metaphorical, fake and temporary. In order to establish the unity of Islam, we must first form and develop the brotherhood of Islam with all of its necessary aspects. This can only be realized through a brotherhood that covers both worlds (the world and the

---

[96] *Ibid.*
[97] Nursi, Said, *Damascus Sermon*, İstanbul: Sözler Neşriyat, 1996, p. 80
[98] *Ibid.*, 81

Hereafter) and receives its support from a Divine source, not through a brotherhood that is based on temporary pleasures of this world.

In light of this, Bediüzzaman interprets the verse, *"The believers are but brothers, so make peace between your brothers; and keep from disobedience to God in reverence for Him and piety (particularly in your duties toward one another as brothers), so that you may be shown mercy,"* (al-Hujurat 49:10) in his Twenty-Second Letter: "[This verse] calls believers to brotherhood [and sisterhood] and mutual love."[99] He adds, "Dispute, discord, partisanship, obstinacy, and envy cause rancor and enmity among believers, and therefore are sins that harm personal, social, and spiritual life. Truth and wisdom, as well as Islam (the viewpoint of supreme humanity) all prove this. Moreover, they poison human life...

It is wrong from the viewpoint of truth. O unjust one who nourishes rancor and enmity for a believer, imagine yourself on a ship or in a house with one criminal and nine innocent persons. If someone tried to destroy the ship or the house (because of that one criminal), you would understand the magnitude of such an injustice and protest. Even if there were one innocent person and nine criminals on that ship, it would still be unjust to sink it.

A believer may be compared to a house or a ship belonging to God. Such a person has not nine, but as many as 20 innocent attributes such as belief, Islam, and neighborliness. If you cherish rancor and enmity for a believer because of one criminal attribute you do not like, and you want to destroy that ship or house created by God, your crime would be most atrocious.

It is wrong from the viewpoint of wisdom. Love and enmity are opposites, like light and darkness, and so their true nature cannot be combined in a single heart. If love is truly felt, hostility assumes the form of pity. Believers should love—and indeed do love—their coreligionists and be pained by any evil seen in them. They should try to improve their coreligionists only with gentleness, for a Prophetic Tra-

---

[99] Nursi, Said, *The Letters*, New Jersey: The Light, 2007, p. 281

dition states: "Believers should not be angry with each other, nor refuse to speak to each other for more than 3 days."[100]

Bediüzzaman prefers using some simple and comprehendible analogies in his works to replace enmity and resentment with solid brotherhood and mutual love which should exist between Muslims. With this thought, he indicates the abundance of commonalities between believers and makes an emphasis on the strengthening factors and on the significance of the elements which impact on brotherhood.

For this reason, the examples he uses when he interprets the verses, removes all doubts from the minds of the readers as they encourage the reader to accept the concept without any questions.

For example: He resembles the act of showing hostility towards a believer who is decorated with Islamic attributes to assuming that small, worthless stones are more valuable than Ka'ba and Mt Uhud. He continues with the following statement: "Unity in belief requires unity of hearts, and oneness of creed demands oneness of society. If you are in the same squadron as someone else, you will feel friendly toward him and so form a mutually friendly relation because you are commanded by one commander. You also will experience a fraternal relationship because you live in the same barracks. Given this, understand your intimate attachment to believers through mutual ties of unity as numerous as the Divine Names, and the bonds of accord and fraternal relations coming from the light and consciousness of belief.

Both of you serve the same One Creator, Sovereign, Object of Worship, Provider... so there are as many ties between you as there are Divine Names. Your Prophet, religion [Islam], and *qibla* are one and the same, and the number of such ties amount to almost a hundred. Your town, country, and state is one, and tens of things are one and the same for you.

These ties require unity and oneness, union and concord, love and brotherhood. Such immaterial chains are strong enough to link all planets together. Preferring something as frail and trivial as a spider's web, which causes dispute, discord, rancor, enmity, and grudges toward fel-

---

[100] *Ibid.*, p. 282

low believers, shows your great disregard for such ties. You seriously offend those causes of love and transgress against those brotherly relationships!"[101]

With the above words, Bediüzzaman encourages and convinces Muslims to unite through faith and stresses on the necessity of abstaining from things that lead to disunity when there are so many commonalities between them.

As it is clear in the explanation above, not only did he advice the brotherhood of Islam but he also intervened and struggled against behaviors that would harm the unity of faith.

His attitude shows us the necessity of standing up bravely for the brotherhood of faith which he had based on solid foundations in his heart and mind.

This is because, he was a believer who had a firm grip on the rope described by the following verse:

> And hold fast, all together, by the rope which God (stretches out for you), and be not divided among yourselves; and remember with gratitude God's favor on you; for ye were enemies and He joined your hearts in love, so that by His Grace, ye became brethren; and ye were on the brink of the pit of Fire, and He saved you from it. Thus doth God make His Signs clear to you: That ye may be guided. (Al Imran 3:103)

By stating, "Yes, the Qur'an is a chain that connects the earth to the heavens; it is the rope of God", with sincerity, he is acknowledging the fact that our century could only be brightened by holding firmly onto this rope and he is also inviting all Muslims to comprehend this reality.

As a natural result of grabbing firmly onto the Holy Qur'an, Bediüzzaman had dedicated his life to serving the Qur'an and sacrificed himself to faith, facing and enduring many difficulties to prevent the disunity of brothers in religion. Moreover, when the opportunity had risen, he never held himself back from screaming out: "the unity of brotherhood in Islam is the right purpose." In order to com-

---

[101] *Ibid.*, p. 282–283

prehend his thoughts about brotherhood, one needs to understand his life, which confirms his words. In all episodes of his life, Bediüzzaman appears as a perfect individual who possesses the very same fundamental qualities. The following statement made by him, is great evidence to this claim: "If I had a hundred honors, I would sacrifice all of them for love and cordiality among my brothers."[102]

The advice of a man, who chooses the wellbeing of his brothers in religion over his own interests, should be appreciated as a compassionate father's struggle to protect his children from the cliffs of destruction that may rise from conflicts in the future or now, hence this advice should be taken seriously. He says: "O my brothers and sisters of the Hereafter, and companions in the service of the Qur'an! You should know—indeed you know—that in this world, and particularly in the services done for the afterlife, a most important foundation, and a greatest power, and a most acceptable intercessor, and a firmest point of reliance, and a shortest way to the truth, and a most answerable prayer, and a most blessed and marvelous means of achieving one's goal, and a most sublime virtue, and a purest form of worship is sincerity, or doing something good or any religious deed purely for God's sake."[103]

It is sincerity that helps us understand the value of brotherhood; prevents us from falling apart due to simple misunderstandings; reminds us of the real enemy—disbelief—which stands on the path of faith and encourages us to work hand in hand and heart to heart without falling into disunity. It invites us to listen to the following Divine Words with passion and to act accordingly: *"And obey God and His Messenger, and do not dispute with one another, or else you may lose heart and your power and energy desert you; and remain steadfast..."* (al-Anfal 8:46).

Bediüzzaman is also quite sensitive in the interpretation of this verse as he focuses on the continuation of the institute of brotherhood: "You should not criticize your brothers and sisters in their service of the Qur'an or belief, and do not provoke their envy by making a display of your attributes. For a person's hands do not compete with

---

[102] Nursi, Said, *The Flashes*, İstanbul: Sözler, 2000, p. 359
[103] Nursi, Said, *The Gleams*, New Jersey: Tughra Books, 2008, p. 225

each other, nor do their eyes criticize one another, nor does their tongue oppose their ears, nor does their heart see the faults of the spirit. Rather, their members complete the deficiencies of one another, veil one another's shortcomings, assist one another in meeting their needs, and help one another with their duties. Otherwise, the life of that person's body would be extinguished, their spirit would go away, and their body would decompose." Then he explains the mystery behind it: "This is because each individual in a true, sincere union can also see with the eyes of the other brothers and sisters, and hear with their ears. It is as if each of the ten persons in true solidarity and unity has the value and power of seeing with twenty eyes, thinking with ten intellects, hearing with twenty ears, and working with twenty hands."[104]

The message he conveys to us is: Muslims should not be heedless masses or crowds, they should be systematic congregations whose hearts have been locked onto to one another. So much so that the pain of a Muslim who has stepped on a thorn should be felt by a Muslim who lives in the other corner of the world.

What Does *Fana fi'l-Ikhwan* Mean?

It is an indispensable sentiment that needs to exist between the members of an ideology which seeks to achieve genuine brotherhood. Bediüzzaman who describes this sentiment as "annihilating yourself between your brothers and preferring their souls over yours" has introduced the term *fana fi'l-ikhwan* into our literature. *Fana fi'l-ikhwan* is a condition in which individuals reach complete perfection in love where they willingly sacrifice all bounties, material and spiritual by preferring other's to their own souls. In short, this condition is defined as *tafani* which means individuals annihilating themselves in one another. Bediüzzaman explains this with the following words:

"As if it were you who possess the merits and virtues of your brothers and sisters, take pride in them and be thankful to God for them.

---

[104] *Ibid.*, pp. 226, 227, 228

The Sufis circulate among themselves such terms as 'annihilation in the guide,' and 'annihilation in the Messenger.' I am not a Sufi, but we should have this principle among ourselves as 'annihilation in the brothers and sisters.' This is called among the brothers and sisters 'mutual annihilation.' It means the brothers and sisters being annihilated in one another. That is to say, oblivious of their own merits and the pride which may arise from them, each person lives with the merits and feelings of their brothers and sisters in their mind. The basis of our way is brotherhood."[105]

"Our way is also the closest friendship. Friendship requires being the closest, most self-sacrificing friend, the most appreciative companion, and the most magnanimous brother or sister." [106]

Certainly, a friendship which originates from the light of faith and flourishes with the flowers of *iman* and takes the transient human being to eternity cannot be compared with any other earthly friendships. *"Those who are intimate friends (in the world) will be enemies one to another on that Day, except the God-revering, pious"* (az-Zukhruf 43:67).

Indeed, those who befriend each other for worldly reasons will leave their friendship on earth when they go. Sometimes, such friendships do not even last on earth. However, friendships formed for God continues on earth and in the life after. Another thing faith gives to humanity is the pure brotherhood that strengthens the bridge between the temporary and the eternal realms. Believers are those who love only for God and condemn only for God. On the Day of Judgment, our Lord will give good news to believers who have organized their lives in accordance with the conditions of brotherhood described above hence prepared themselves for the Hereafter: *"O My servants! You will have no fear today, nor will you grieve!"* (az-Zukhruf 43:68).

Is the good news of this Divine revelation not worth enduring the burdens that come from our brothers in this short life? Is it not worth taking our time to correct the mistakes of our brothers? Or, is it not worth refraining from insignificant rivalries on the road to our

---

[105] *Ibid.*, p. 229
[106] *Ibid.*

true goal? It is worth the trouble a hundred times over! Let us listen to Bediüzzaman: "O my brothers and sisters! Our way which we try to follow in the service of the wise Qur'an is based on truth and requires true brotherhood. Brotherhood requires self- annihilation among the brothers and sisters and preferring them to oneself. Therefore, there should not be rivalry among us that arises from seeking status in people's eyes."[107]

The reason for this is, just as *iman* gives life to the heart, brotherhood in religion gives life to society. Bediüzzaman presented *fana fi'l-ikhwan* as a principle of life and emphasized the significance of this mutual support between brothers with the following words:

Life is the product of unity and oneness. When harmonious unity departs, so does the spiritual life. As the Divine verse indicates, the congregation loses its jubilation in the absence of order: *"And obey God and His Messenger, and do not dispute with one another, or else you may lose heart and your power and energy desert you; and remain steadfast. Surely, God is with those who remain steadfast"* (al-Anfal 8:46).

"If three 1's do not unite or come together, they will have only the value of 3. But if they unite or come together, they will gain the value of 111. Four separate 4's make 16. But if they come together in true brotherhood, along the same line for the fulfillment of the same duty, they will have the value of the power of 4444. History records numerous events which bear witness to the fact that 16 self-sacrificing people in true brotherhood have obtained the moral strength of more than 4000 people."[108]

The difference between unity and disunity is quite obvious for all of us. However, knowing something and practicing it are different things. The believers know the necessity of helping each other, sharing the workload of servanthood, mutual support on the path of righteousness and the importance of refraining from disunity due to personal gains. However, implementing it and making a decision on how to protect themselves from conflicts is not that easy.

---

[107] *Ibid.*, p. 233
[108] *Ibid.*, pp. 227–228

In response to faith, one should also uncover the secrets of behaving without falling into the tricks of the devil and following the temptations of the world and the carnal desire. This secret is: preferring your brother over yourself; choosing sincerity over rivalry and the Hereafter over worldly contentment. In relation to this, Bediüzzaman says: "Prefer the souls of your brothers and sisters to your own in honor, position, public approval, and even in things like the material benefits of which the carnal soul is enamored."[109]

On another occasion, he states: "Do not open the doors of criticism to each other. There are many things to be criticized outside the circle of your brotherhood. Just as I feel proud of the qualities you possess, feel happy that you have them and also consider them to be mine, you should also evaluate each other as the way your master does. Each one of you should be a promoter of the other's virtues.[110]

READING TEXT

The Best Human Being Is a Person
Who Could Even Be Friends with Cobras

Fethullah Gülen explains the importance of brotherhood amongst people who follow the same path: "It is imperative that our friends in this sanctified circle work together in harmony. In the light of the Qur'an's indication and caution: *"We cause you (O humankind) to be a means of testing for one another"* (al-Furqan 25:20) and *"...in order to try you by means of one another"* (Muhammad 47:4) as we are tested with others, we are also tested amongst ourselves. Of course, such testing will earn us different types of Divine rewards.

In this regard, I would say from my perspective, people who have the best manners are those who could even establish relationships with the most cranky by adjusting their behaviors according to these individuals. Previously, when I explained this topic, I had said: "The best of human beings are those who could even befriend cobras!"

---

[109] *Ibid.*, p. 229
[110] Hümeyra, Ayşe, "Bediüzzaman ve fena fi'l-ihvan," *Yeni Ümit*, number 46, p. 37

I ask you, are we lower than Hindu monks that we cannot get along with each other when they could even make friends with cobras! Considering that we are gathered around a sanctified thought.

We are people who should be mannered with the manners of the Messenger of God, yet if we are feeling uncomfortable and failing to get along with others due to their oddities, then we need to reexamine our own manners in the treatment room of the conscience. And again, in my perspective, if these people who have dedicated themselves to the service are not getting along with their friends in this sanctified circle, then either they are mental patients or they are egocentrics who victimize others in the lens of their own souls.

So, for the love of God, let us not look for faults in people whom we share the same path, especially in such a time when there is a great need for individuals of all levels and status, in the cause of faith and the Qur'an. Let us not speak against anyone and stop others from speaking behind our brothers. As explained many times before, let us act like prosecutors to our carnal selves and defend others like a lawyer. In this thought, let us all say to ourselves:

"You are a traitor who has released himself to heedlessness. You are a slothful person who cannot leave his house without getting seven hours of sleep. You are a prisoner of the flesh, a slave and servant of your own body."

Yes, we should always say this and see others as angels. May God soften our hearts and give us success in embracing everyone, beginning with our brothers."[111]

QUESTIONS

1. What is the title given to the brotherhood established between the Ansar of Medina and the Muhajirin of Mecca by the noble Prophet?
   a. *Muakhat*
   b. *Musawat*
   c. *Mutaqabiliyat*
   d. *Mujazat*

---

[111] Gülen, M. Fethullah, *Fasıldan Fasıla-3*, İstanbul. Nil, 2011, p. 78

2. In the Surah Humaza, "Wow to those who engage in *humaza* and *lumaza*," what do the terms "*humaza*" and "*lumaza*" mean?
   a. Those who do not pray
   b. Those who do not give alms
   c. Those who belittle others; speak behind their backs and make fun of them with facial gestures
   d. Those who will remain in hell for eternity

3. Fill in the blank in the following statement: "O my brothers and sisters of the Hereafter, and companions in the service of the Qur'an! You should know—indeed you know—that in this world, and particularly in the services done for the after-life, a most important foundation, and a greatest power, and a most acceptable intercessor, and a firmest point of reliance, and a shortest way to the truth, and a most answerable prayer, and a most blessed and marvelous means of achieving one's goal, and a most sublime virtue, and a purest form of wor-ship is ...., or doing something good or any religious deed purely for God's sake."
   a. Worship
   b. Reciting the Qur'an
   c. Fasting
   d. Sincerity

4. Which of the below is not a virus that threatens brotherhood?
   a. Thinking of your brother before yourself)
   b. False assumption
   c. Spying on others' privacy
   d. Envy or jealousy

5. In relation to the term *ukhuwah*, which of the below is wrong?
   a. It comes from Arabic.
   b. It is used for biological brothers or sisters.
   c. It means brotherhood.
   d. It comes from the word *akh* which means brother.

6. What does *fana fi'l-ikhwan* mean?
   a. *Tafani*, being annihilated in the brother

b. Wishing for a bad thing for a brother in faith

c. Explaining the mistakes and faults of a brother in faith

d. Belittling or degrading a Muslim individual

7. Which word describes the act of wishing for a beautiful quality that your brother possesses to be yours and wishing that it is removed from him.

a. Competition

b. Ambition

c. Covetousness

d. Greed

8. "In this regard, I would say from my perspective, people who have the best manners are those who could even establish relationships with the most cranky by adjusting their behaviors according to these individuals." What is the main emphasis in this statement?

a. The necessity of brotherhood

b. The importance of knowing the Qur'an and Sunnah

c. One should refrain from bad-tempered people.

d. One should protect himself from evil people.

5

ALTRUISM AND MUNIFICENCE

A ltruism means to discard and sacrifice one's self, possessions and wealth, and even honor and dignity for a higher purpose and ideals. Altruistic munificence is a higher level of generosity where one thinks of others without any personal expectations and considers the benefits of others more than his own.

In fact, altruism, a condition of self-sacrifice is a behavior which is exhibited by almost all creatures in the universe. In essence, it is a beautiful behavior, however, depending on how and where it is used, it will produce different results. Whilst the living organisms that have no self-consciousness practice this without knowing, human beings are required to practice it through the use of their freewill and as the way it was prescribed by religion.

A mother spends sleepless nights for her children whilst a soldier does the same for his nation. The heart of a mother and a father beat like a drum as they feel concerned about their child's wellbeing. Moreover, for parents, self-sacrifice in the name of their child is not a big deal at all. A teacher delivers or conveys his knowledge which he had gathered with extreme care, like a bee collecting nectar from a thousand flowers, to his students without any complaints. A person should be prepared to display all types of self-sacrifice for his friend and almost all human beings display such behavior when it becomes necessary.

A believer, on the other hand, displays his altruism for his servanthood before all. The Prayers offered without any concern for the cold or the hot weather, and also without any regards for the early morning hours or the late hours of the night. Fasting observed without thinking about the cold winter days or the hot summer days. Putting aside a part of your precious wealth so that it may be distributed to the poor and the needy as *zakah*; and just because He commanded, sacrificing your wealth and health to respond to the call of your Lord by performing Hajj; and the act of "enjoining good and forbidding evil" (*amr bi al-maruf wa nayh an al-munkar*) and its furthest point which is going to battles and having no concern for your own life. These are all part of a servanthood which can only set sail with the ship of altruism.[112]

Moreover, running to the aid of human beings as individuals and as a community, and abstaining from physical and spiritual pleasures in the name of spreading the message of our exalted religion is also a form of altruism.

How Can We Become an Altruistic Person?

An altruist, in a true sense will sacrifice everything he has, loves and values without any hesitation, when the necessity arises. Furthermore, he would abandon his own gains and endure all types of difficulties in order to help his brother by preferring him over himself. As a matter of fact, those who do not have a concern for others as they have for their own problems are destitute of a sensitive soul. This beautiful manner of altruism is the most significant quality that separate believers from the others. In essence, altruism is a way of life which originates from the power of faith.

A beloved servant of God, who has adopted altruism as a second nature, will be sensitive towards everything that occurs around him. He will drop the notion of "fire burns where it falls" and will act on the idea of "no matter where it falls, it will first burn me." Such a person will be responsible for all the people around the world who are being oppressed, tyrannized, tormented, and left starving in poverty and in tears hence he would try to reach out to them.

[112] Ünsal, Ali, "Fedakarlık," http://www.herkul.org/index.php/dusunce-helezonu/yazarlar/281-Fedakarlik

In his vocabulary, the terms "I do not care" or "what is it to me" do not exist. He rejects all excuses that involve the following arguments "I am also a person in need. There are many people who have the means and power to solve these issues. Let them think about it and find a solution." He makes the effort to become the virtuous person that the Qur'an mentions:

> If only there had been among the generations before you (of whom some We destroyed) people with lasting qualities (such as faith, knowledge, virtue, and good deeds, whose goal was what is lasting with God, the eternal life of the Hereafter, and) who would warn against disorder and corruption on earth! Among them only a few, included among those whom We saved, did this. But those who did wrong (against God by associating partners with Him, or against transgressing His commands, or against people by violating their rights) were lost in the pursuit of pleasures without scruples, and were criminals committed to accumulating sins. (Hud, 11:116)

Our Lord will reward those who display this type of beautiful altruistic behavior with pleasant blessings on earth and with unimaginable eternal bounties in the life after. The following verse indicates to this reality:

> For those who do good, aware that God is seeing them, is the best (of the rewards that God has promised for good deeds), and still more. Neither stain nor ignominy will cover their faces. They are the companions of Paradise; they will abide therein. (Yunus 10:26)

For some people altruism is "My comfort and needs come first. I will help others when my needs are fulfilled." Such perspective of life does not concur with the notion of altruism defined by the Qur'an. The reason for this is these people donate from the material possessions that they do not need anymore. What they give have no value for them, because it does not affect their wealth.

Such people may consider themselves as philanthropists. No doubt, giving in such manner should also be considered as good behavior. However, it cannot be considered as true altruism. The manners that God is pleased with are described clearly in the Qur'an "when necessary, sacrificing all wealth and giving away the things that one loves the most." In relation to this the Holy Qur'an defines the true essence of altruism as: *"You will never be able to attain godliness and virtue until you spend of what you love (in God's cause, or to provide sustenance for the needy). Whatever you spend, God has full knowledge of it"* (Al Imran 3:92).

READING TEXT
The Characteristics of the Altruistic
and Self-Sacrificing Souls

According to Fethullah Gülen, an important element of the duty of *irshad* and *tabligh* is "giving up on living with pleasure and letting live." This is defined as self-sacrifice. It is impossible for a nation or a society to revive itself in a real sense unless it is formed by individuals whose hearts are filled with the feelings of altruism, self-sacrifice and sincerity. As the noble Messenger of God left behind nothing in the name of worldly possessions, so too Abu Bakr had no material wealth to be divided amongst those he left behind. When Umar received the fatal blow from a dagger, he said: "Can you check if I have enough to pay my debts? If it is not enough, get a loan from the sons of Adiyy and if they do not have it either, get a loan from the Quraysh and pay what I owe."[113] This was his dying wish.

Gülen says: "A person who only thinks of himself is either not a human being or he is an incomplete human being. The path that goes to true humanity passes from neglecting oneself whilst thinking of others." He also explains the different dimensions of altruism with the following words: "One should be a prosecutor when it comes to his own faults, but a lawyer when it comes to others. A perfect human being is a person who says "after you" even when he is released from hell or when he walks into paradise. Regardless of the conditions, a true human being is a person who does not leave his neighbor's container empty as he fills his own container with milk."[114]

A person's degree by the side of God is measured according to his munificence and altruism. And the most evident sign of munifi-

---

[113] Gülen, M. Fethullah, *Fasıldan Fasıla-1*, İzmir: Nil, 1997, p. 65
[114] Gülen, M. Fethullah, *Ölçü veya Yoldaki Işıklar*, İstanbul, Nil, 2011, p. 136

cence and altruism is sacrificing your own pleasures and joy for the happiness of others. I wonder if one could imagine an altruism that is bigger than throwing your own dignity and honor under your feet, swallowing your anger even in situations where you should be roaring like a lion and restricting your own happiness by limiting your needs for the salvation and wellbeing of your society.[115]

Fethullah Gülen describes the qualities of altruistic souls: "Those who run on the path to enlightening humanity, those who struggle to make others happy and lend a hand to them at the various abysses of life are exalted souls who have comprehended themselves. These souls behave like guardian angels in society as they battle against all the calamities that have engulfed their people. They stand before gale storms, walk into infernos and wait cautiously, prepared for possible tremors that may occur."[116]

One Should Only Be Self-Sacrificing for the Sake of God

All forms of philanthropy should be done with sincerity and supported individuals or society should not be left in obligation. True altruism will only be accomplished by targeting the pleasure of God and without expecting anything from people. God talks about such servants in the Qur'an:

> Those who spend their wealth in God's cause and then do not follow up what they have spent with putting (the receiver) under obligation and taunting, their reward is with their Lord, and they will have no fear, nor will they grieve. (al-Baqarah 2:262)

Another verse mentions the sincere attitude of believers who display altruism only for the sake of God: *"(Rather, he spends) only in longing for the good pleasure of his Lord, the Most High. He will certainly be contented (he with his Lord and his Lord with him)"* (al-Layl, 92:20–21).

On the other hand, another verse describes the situation of those who refrain from giving because they fear poverty and state that on

---

[115] *Ibid.,*
[116] *Ibid.,* p. 230

the Day of Judgment these people will offer everything they have and had saved as compensation so that they could save themselves from punishment. However, their offers and negotiations will not be accepted.[117]

The Noble Prophet Represented Altruism at the Highest Level

Altruism and self-sacrifice are one of the most important qualities of a person of *tabligh*. Those who do not take altruism into account right from the beginning will never reach their objectives. Those who are prepared to spend everything they have, material and spiritual, when it becomes necessary, will certainly reach their goal and sit at the pinnacle of altruism.

Our noble Prophet is a guide who holds the highest rank in altruism. His entire life has been woven with altruism. For this reason, he has sacrificed his wealth, health and personal needs for the salvation of humanity. As he laid the foundations of religion in Mecca, first he commenced with himself and then those around him as he injected the spirit of altruism to all human beings. He explained altruism at the highest level as he practiced it himself.

Khadija, for example, the wife of the noble Messenger of God had spent everything she had on the path of this noble mission which she believed in without putting the sultan of the both worlds in a situation where he had to ask for her support. The expenditure of all the dinners and banquets given to polytheists of Mecca who were invited to Islam was financed by Khadija. Our fortunate mother, who was one of the wealthiest persons in Mecca before Islam, did not have enough money to purchase her burial cloth at the time of her death.

The Companions Were Racing with Each Other in Altruism

The Companions who were taught by the noble Prophet had also displayed an inimitable spirit of altruism as they lived exemplary lives. In

---

[117] See Rad 13:18

every period of their lives they had shown an effort and exertion with feelings of altruism as they left behind their homes, families, wealth, work and dignity, when it was necessary, to defend the security and unity of Muslims.

Within the Companions, one of the altruistic souls who hold a special place is Abu Talha al-Ansari. He is a Companion well known for his altruism in the name of God. As much as being an altruist, he was also a brave soldier who defended the Prophet with his life during the battle of Uhud. He was a great archer who formed a living shield in front of the Prophet at Uhud. As he did this, he shouted "Do not worry, O Messenger of God, they cannot harm you before they martyr me." In turn, the noble Messenger honored him with the following words, "Within the army, the roar of Abu Talha is more blessed than a thousand men."[118]

Abu Talha and his wife Umm Sulaym had a different place in the heart of the noble Messenger of God. He would visit this family frequently and honored them. They would offer him whatever they had in their house. The noble Prophet had a share of whatever that was cooked in this house.[119] Their behavior showed that they were kind, sensitive individuals who understood people's situations and displayed an exemplary altruism by sharing whatever they had.

The first addresses of Islam were the Companions of the Messenger of God; therefore, their attitudes towards the revelation and the *hadith* were quite important from the point of comprehending and practicing the Divine commandments and the message of the noble Prophet, and also from the perspective of becoming role models for the following generations. In this regard, Talha was a perfect example for the following generations. The reason for this is he had comprehended the messages that invited him to altruism and implemented them in a most beautiful way.

According to Anas ibn Malik, Talha was the wealthiest person amongst the Ansar of Medina. His favored property was the garden

---

[118] Ibn Hajar, *Isaba*, p. 1081
[119] Ibn Sa'd, *Tabakat*, 3/504

of Bayruha which was located across the Masjid an-Nabawi. The Messenger of God would frequently visit this garden and drink from the sweet water there.

When the verse, *"You will never be able to attain godliness and virtue until you spend of what you love (in God's cause, or to provide sustenance for the needy). Whatever you spend, God has full knowledge of it"* (Al Imran 3:92) was revealed, Abu Talha came to the noble Messenger and said: "O Messenger of God; God says that unless we give what we love the most, we cannot become righteous. I love my garden Bayruha and I am giving it away as a charity. O Messenger of God, make use of it for the sake of God. The noble Messenger replied: "Well done Abu Talha! This is a profitable deal. I heard what you said but I suggest that you leave this property to your relatives." Abu Talha said: "I will do this O Messenger of God." He then distributed the property amongst his relatives and his cousins.[120]

As it is seen, our Prophet was quite pleased by the fact that he had taken the message of the verse and displayed his altruism accordingly.

Abu Hurairah explains that one day a man came to the Prophet and said: "I am hungry." The noble Messenger sent a message to one of his wives and requested something to eat. His wife replied: "O Messenger of God, there is nothing but water in the house." The Messenger of God then requested the same thing from his other wife, she replied the same way: "By the One who sent you as a Messenger, there is nothing but water in the house!" Upon hearing this, the noble Prophet addressed his Companions and said: "Who would like to invite this person to their house tonight?" A person from the Ansar said: "I can take him as a guest O Messenger of God! Then he took the poor person to his house. As he entered the house, he asked his wife: "Is there anything to eat?" His wife replied: "No, there is only enough food for the children." The Companion said to his wife: "Put the children to bed. Then turn off the oil-lamp when the guest comes into the room. We will sit down and pretend that we are eating as well." The guest ate while they went to bed with empty stomachs. The next

---

[120] *Sahih al-Bukhari*, Wasaya, 17; Zakah, 44; Ashriba 13; Tafsir as-surah 3/5

morning when that Companion came to the Masjid an-Nabawi, our noble Prophet said to him: "God was pleased with what you have done for your visitor last night."[121]

In another narration of this *hadith*, there is an indication that the following verse was revealed after the incident:

> Those who, before their coming, had their abode (in Medina, preparing it as a home for Islam and faith, love those who emigrate to them for God's sake, and in their hearts do not begrudge what they have been given; and (indeed) they prefer them over themselves, even though poverty be their own lot. (They, too, have a share in such gains of war.) Whoever is guarded against the avarice of his own soul—those are the ones who are truly prosperous. (al-Hashr 59:9)[122]

The society needs people who are unselfish, altruist and ready to share whatever they have at all times. Such people should be praised and valued by the society.

What an Immense Profit Suhayb Made

Suhayb lived in Musul with his family when he was young. He was taken as a prisoner by the Romans at a very young age and then sold to the sons of Kalb who later brought him to Mecca. The collar of slavery was placed around his neck. Sometime later, Abdullah ibn Jud'an purchased and emancipated him. However, he decided that he would stay by the side of Abdullah for the rest of his life.

When he heard the invitation of the Prophet, he went to ibn Arqam's house with Ammar ibn Yasir and embraced Islam. He was one the believers who was weak and had no family to protect him thus he faced many tortures and persecution.

One day, great opportunity to migrate came his way. This was a chance that would save him from his troubles and suffering.

---

[121] *Sahih al-Bukhari*, Menakıbu'l-ansar, 10; Tafsir as-surah 59/6; *Sahih Muslim*, Ashriba 172
[122] *Ibid.*

He made his mind up and left Mecca to travel to Medina. However, the Quraysh had heard about it and they were not going to let him migrate from Mecca. They stood on his path and said:

"When you came to us, you had nothing hence you were in a terrible condition. Whatever you earned, you earned it amongst us. Now, you intend to take your wealth and leave us, do you really think that we are going to allow this? We will never permit this!"

At first, Suhayb stared at them for awhile. They thought that if they took his possessions away from him, he might change his mind. These people who had no other values than worldly materials did not even think about values that even the entire world would be sacrificed for. Suhayb said to them: "O the people of Quraysh! You know that I am the best archer amongst you! I will release my arrows upon you and you will not come near me until I run out of arrows. Then I will use my sword until it is broken into small pieces. However, if your target is not me but my wealth, I will show you where I keep it, you may do as you wish with it."

They replied: "Show us the location of your wealth and will leave you alone!"

Their hunger for worldly possessions was incomprehensible. In shock, he asked again: "Will you let me go if I leave all my wealth to you?"

They replied: "yes we will" in a sarcastic manner. They never thought such a thing would occur. However, Suhayb was quite serious as he said: "Ok then, my entire wealth is yours."

They were all in shock. How could a man leave his entire wealth behind and run to Muhammad? In reality, this was an astonishing situation for them and it was something that cannot be comprehended through Quraysh mentality. The news of Suhayb's gallantry had reached the noble Prophet.

Immediately, he said: "What an immense profit Suhayb has made!"[123] The noble Messenger of God praised Suhayb for his behavior and mentioned his sacrifice to everyone. In essence, the Divine Message brought

---

[123] Ibn Kathir, *al-Bidaya*, 3/173

by Gabriel was screaming out the profits by this trade: *"And (in contrast, there is) among the people one who sells himself in pursuit of God's good pleasure. God is All-Pitying towards His servants (and therefore commends to them reverent piety and fear of His punishment)"* (al-Baqarah 2:207)[124]

READING TEXT

He Sacrificed His Life for His Friend

The brotherhood and loyalty between the believers was best displayed in action during the era of the contentment. They had written the most valuable golden pages of history which no man shall ever accomplish again. Their attributes defined as *ithar* was mentioned by the Holy Qur'an:

> Those who, before their coming, had their abode (in Medina, preparing it as a home for Islam and faith, love those who emigrate to them for God's sake, and in their hearts do not begrudge what they have been given; and (indeed) they prefer them over themselves, even though poverty be their own lot. (They, too, have a share in such gains of war.) Whoever is guarded against the avarice of his own soul—those are the ones who are truly prosperous. (al-Hashr 59:9)

In the exegesis of the Holy Qur'an, this is explained as "Give your brother preference over yourself in nobility, rank, honor and even material gains which your nature loves." This reality was lived in every era of our gracious history which evidently holds many living examples.

There are also many examples of this fidelity and altruism during the era of the Babur Empire. In the beginning of the 16th Century, Babur Shah and his grandchildren who ruled the region of what is India and Pakistan today, have served faith immensely. Bayram Khan, who was a famous and valuable commander in this Turkic Islamic nation, displayed many examples of bravery. During the many battles

---

[124] See al-Baqarah 2:207

with the Afghanis, he achieved consecutive victories but on one occasion he was captured as a prisoner of war.

Initially, the Afghan commander treated him kindly. He even thought of releasing him because of his legendry bravery. However, one day, Bayram Khan acted in a careless manner and disclosed his plans to defeat the Afghans. From that point on, the treatment he had been receiving took a drastic turn. Instead of releasing him, they decided to execute Bayram Khan.

Bayram Khan sensed the decision and made a plan to escape with a man named Kasım Bey. They succeeded in their escape. However, when the Afghani soldiers realized that they were gone, they sent a search party after them. Before long, they were recaptured. The Afghan soldiers had received orders to kill Bayram Khan on sight, but they could not tell who was who. Finally, they decided on Kasım Bey who had a bigger built than Bayram Khan. So they prepared to execute him.

Upon seeing this, Bayram Khan became quite emotional as he did not want his friend to be killed in his place. He shouted at the commander of the team: "You are making a big mistake! Do not kill him, he is not Bayram, I am!"

Kasım Bey, on the other hand, was not saying anything as he had already accepted his fate. Upon hearing the words of Bayram Khan, he intervened and denied his claim. He could not let them kill the commander of Babur army. He believed that Bayram Khan would serve his nation better than he. With the feelings of *ithar* that had been embroidered into all the entire cells in his body, he stood up as he pointed at Bayram Khan and calmly said: "Look at this loyal servant! He is trying to save me by sacrificing his own life! I urge you to let him go, he is just a poor servant who is pretending to be Bayram Khan!"

The Afghan commander believed Kasım Bey as he had spoken serenely and without any hesitation. He then ordered the release of Bayram Bey. The great commander whom they feared for many years was walking away as Kasım Bey was being executed. Kasım Bey would go into the pages of history as a perfect example of fidelity and self-sacrifice.

Our History is Ample with Such Fidelity and Altruism

Just like in the Age of Happiness, the lives of our glorious forefathers who had taken the Companions as an example to themselves have also produced many pictures of fidelity and altruism.

National Resistance is the name of a struggle of fight to death. During this fight to death, the people of Anatolia had written a legendry story of revival as they defended this beautiful land which has been kneaded for centuries with the sound of *adhan*, from the enemy boots that tried to march on it.

In this battle to protect the rosy color of our flag from fading, we see many Mehmetçiks, Ayşeciks and Fatmacıks whose natural disposition have been molded with gallantry. Most of them are the unknown heroes of this people.

It was during those days that the earth squirted martyrs and many suns had set for the sake of a crescent. It was a period in which we observe the boiling of Anatolia and a feverish action taking place all over the land. Everyone is at the front lines, from a grey-bearded old man to a young man whose facial hair has not grown yet. Indeed, anyone who is able to hold a gun was there. There was only one objective: To prevent this land from an invasion. However, this mission was difficult as it needed blood, sweat and tears.

In this Anatolia of scarcity where everyone had taken on a duty depending on their ability, one of our mothers, whose name is memorized by the inhabitants of the heavens, was running from one front to the other as she carried ammunitions to our soldiers. She would not even stop to think about her feeble and weak body as she moved continuously.

It was on one freezing morning in Kastamonu where the soldiers at the military barracks woke up to an astonishing scene. This saintly woman was standing outside with her hands raised in a position as if she was praying. She was not moving. It was a surprising picture; what was she doing outside in freezing conditions of the morning? As few soldiers walked towards the old woman to invite her inside so that she could warm herself, they came face to face with an incredible reality. This saintly woman, whose eyes pierced through your soul, had used the only blanket she had, to cover the ammunition thus she had frozen to death with her arms raised like a statue.

Later, they asked who she was but no one knew her identity. The only information they could get their hands on was that she was a woman from the village of Şeydiler. Like many other noble but unknown heroes, they entrusted her body to the bosom of this sanctified land.[125]

The common name of these unsung heroes was Mehmetçik hence many noble women like her had rushed to the frontlines and struggled with blood and tears to serve their nation. Then without being rewarded for their services, they dispersed the seeds of spring and went away as unknown Fatmacıks and Ayşeciks.

Let us provide another example: It was a rainy autumn night in 1915. The Gallipoli Campaign had been won but the war with seven different nations who had their eyes on the sacred values of this nation continued. The city of Bilecik, the emergence point of the great Ottoman State which was once dubbed as "The Eternal State" was hosting a different kind of activity. A group of young men whose facial hair had not even grown yet were boarding a train with an intention to fight the foreigners who had come to invade their land.

The whistle signifying that the train was about to move had blown and the station became extremely active. The lighting that kept on striking was brightening the silhouette of an old Turkish mother. This woman who stood in the rain and cold with determination was noticed by the military commander Abdülkadir Bey who felt a sense of respect and admiration for her. Quickly he ran towards her and asked if she needed anything. The old woman straightened up like a soldier and explained that she was the mother of Hüseyin the son of Mehmet from the village of Akgünlü and added that she had come to see her lion off the battle.

The commander wished to get the prayer of this sanctified woman whose face had collected centuries of burdens. Quickly he summoned

---

[125] Refik, İbrahim, *Geçmişten Geleceğe Işıklar*, İstanbul: Albatros, 2000, p. 84

for Hüseyin. The young man came running and grabbed the blessed hands of his mother.

The despaired mother embraced her son for one last time with great passion and compassion and then made the following historical statement: "Hüseyin, my brave son; your uncle was martyred at Şıpka, your father at Dömeke and just eight months ago, your brothers were martyred at Çanakkale. You are my last fragment! However, I will not bless the milk I had given to you if the sound of *adhan* ceases from the minarets and if the lamps of the mosques go out. Give your life and do not return! If you pass from Şıpka, do not forget to recite al-Fatiha to your uncle. May God help you on your journey!"

This is an advice given by a mother to her only living son. The commander was frozen like a statue upon hearing these words from this blessed mother. He asked "Was all your family members martyred?"

The reply given by this mother who should be a crown on our heads had sent shivers down the spine of the commander: "Not just my family... for the past fifty years; our village cemetery had not witnessed the burial of a man. So what if we all die, let our nation survive!" She was an Anatolian mother.

Let us give an example of another unnamed mother who lived in the same era: It was a period in which our blessed nation was facing one calamity after another. There was smell of blood and gun powder all around land. From young men to girls who prepared for their weddings and from grey-breaded old men to covered grandmothers, everyone had sworn an oath to fight for their nation until the days promised by God would come.

It was in one of these days we hear the squeaking sound of an ox-cart. It is as if the wheels were screaming out the words, "Do not let dirty hands touch my sacred land!" It was the region of İnebolu and a mother walking bare feet was carrying her child in a blanket as she pulled on her ox-cart which was loaded with ammunition. Her feet which were covered in corns were making historical marks on this blessed land.

This was a unique picture no artist could ever depict. Suddenly, the drops of mercy began to turn into heavy rain as if it was giving the news of a joyous spring. What followed had made the picture even more remarkable. The mother removed the blanket from the tiny body of her baby and covered the ammunition so that it did not get wet. O Lord, what kind of a faith is this!

I do know if angels gathered to protect the baby from the heavy rain but a few hours later, they reached a public house in Ilgaz. It was the middle of the night.

A weak hand knocked on the huge doors and shouted: "Open the doors!"

A few minutes later the owner of the hotel replied: "There is no room!"

The woman shouted again and uttered something that would be written in the books of history with golden letters: "I can sleep outside with my baby but you must take the ammunition in and keep it in a safe place!"

These were the mothers who gave birth to the legendry Mehmetçiks who defended out nation.

It was during those days that the door of Cemal Bey, who was the governor of one of our border cities, was being knocked by the gendarme in the late hours of the night. As he opened the door a soldier informed him that a woman from a village which was divided between Russia and Türkiye was requesting to be accepted as a refugee. She was refusing to go back no matter how much they had insisted.

They brought the poor woman into the governor's office and as soon as she saw Cemal Bey, she fell onto her knees and began to beg. She was weeping as she explained her story. Upon hearing the things she was explaining, Cemal Bey's admiration and respect for this woman began to increase by the minute.

This mother, who has been molded with the mentality of her people and religion, was pregnant. She had concealed her pregnancy for seven months, hiding in the mountains and eating leaves and grass. A few days before her due date for birth, she crossed the border into Turkish territory.

Her only wish was to give birth to her child in her mother land and then leave her baby to the authorities and go back. If she stayed in the Russian territory, her baby would be taken by the Russian authorities.

A mother whose heart was burning with such a noble desire could not be turned away hence the governor did what was necessary and accepted her refugee status. The virtuous mother delivered her baby within a week and after embracing her child for awhile she gave him to the authorities and returned her village.

Yes, these mothers who sent their beloved children to the front-lines in those days are again sending their sons and daughters all over the world. How fortunate are these heroes of compassion!

READING TEXT
Mehmet Akif's Altruism Bring Tears to Our Eyes

Our national poet, Mehmet Akif is a friend of God who believed and lived the values he believed in, and a man who made his place in history. The following incident that would even draw the envy of the inhabitants of the Arabian Desert sky would be a great example for Akif's dedication and sincerity to practice his religion:

It was the years in which Akif visited Hijaz with Eşref Kuşcubaşı, the chief of intelligence. They were at the Al-Muazzam train station of Hijaz. This was a station in the middle of the desert where there were no other buildings, greenery, water, human beings or animals. The entire station was made up of a small waiting room and a tiny house where the station master and his wife lived. The conditions in which the station master lived were awful. The only thing they had in the room was a pillow made out of straws. There were no chairs, tables or couches. The station master's wife was pregnant and she was due in a few days time. The poor man was helpless as he asked Mehmet Akif and Eşref Bey: "Do you have any old clothes so that we could use them as a blanket for the baby?"

There was a sign of great grief on Akif's face as he spoke to Eşref Bey: "It is imperative that we help this woman. There is a serious risk here; this baby's life is in danger. Perhaps, I could go to Damascus and bring a few things from there." Eşref Bey replied: "No Akif, the return trip would take at least five days. We have been travelling in the desert for months now. You must be exhausted. How could you handle this trip?"

Akif said: "Exhaustion is not an issue, there is a tragedy here. Do you even know what extreme poverty is? My heart cannot carry the burden of this family."

Akif recited the *basmala* and left for Damascus. Five days later he returned with many things he had purchased. He was extremely fatigued when he came to Al-Muazzam yet the pleasure of fulfilling a duty was evident on his face. Some years later, Eşref Bey analyzed the incident:

"O blessed Akif! In order to help a woman in poverty, you travelled for five days without proper sleep and in cargo trains when you had already been under the intense sixty-three degrees of desert heat for many months.[126]

What Does Sacrificing from One's Feelings of Material and Spiritual *Fuyud* Mean?

Fuyud (or *fuyuzat*) means an increase, prosperity, opulence, blessings and it is the plural form of *fayd*. The term *fayd* means inspirations that help the development of spiritual life and deepening of one's inner world. In the life after, *fayd* defined as blessings that result in reaching the eternal paradise, earning the pleasure of God and beholding His beauty. In general, we should understand the word *fayd* as spiritual pleasure and contentment.

Material feelings of *fuyud* can be defined as one's lawful desires to attain pleasure and contentment. Eating and drinking without going into extremes and benefitting from what is made lawful by God and consuming His blessings and bounties is a right granted to human beings. Moreover, they are a necessity of being human.

However, these benefits have a limit. For example, benefiting from what is not rightfully yours or from things that religion does not permit is not a right thing to do. God is not pleased with such behavior. Human beings have a right to benefit from whatever God deemed as

---

[126] *Ibid.*, p. 84

lawful and appropriate for His servants. If a servant wishes, he has the right to benefit from these blessings or if he wishes he could save them for future generation and let them benefit from his rightful blessings.

Spiritual feelings of *fuyud*, on the other hand, can be defined as living with the dream of entering paradise and benefitting from its bounties and a desire for metaphysical pleasures. Having faith in God and learning His Divine Names and attributes provides a deep pleasure for the heart and the soul. There are unique pleasures in being close to God that can never be attained from worldly pleasures. On the road that begins with belief in God and continues with His love, there are surprises in every step.

The pleasures experienced on this path are called spiritual feelings of *fuyud*. Sometimes these travelers can even go further and experience some unique phenomena and blessings which were granted only to saintly servants. Or one could receive so much pleasure from worship that he would feel as if he is living paradise on earth as he takes a sip of pleasure from everything he offers in the name of servanthood.

These are pleasures that one feels with his spirituality and the heart. Even a drop of these pleasures would be preferred over all the material pleasures on earth. Yes, a drop of pleasure felt with the heart and the soul would surpass a thousand pleasures of the flesh and the body.

Consequently, when we mention sacrificing from one's material and spiritual feelings of *fuyud*, we are talking about a sacrifice made from both material and spiritual pleasures by devoted souls who prefer their ideals over their pleasures. A soul that has committed itself to an ideal would withdraw his hands from all forms of feelings of *fuyud*; he does not make them an objective or an aim for himself. Besides the sacrifice from things that should be sacrificed by this person for his ideals, it is also expected of him to make a sacrifice from the things which he does not need to give. This kind of behavior is a necessity of being a devoted soul.

As you would know, Bediüzzaman mentions the issue of "abdication" in various chapters of his works. As he describes the path of impotence, deficiency, zeal, gratitude, compassion and contemplation, he touches on the fundamental principles of "abdication" which is embraced by the Naqshbandi School of Sufism. On the path of the school of Muhammad Bahauddin Naqshband, one needs to abandon four things. These things are described with the following famous Persian lines:

> *Dar tariqi Naqshibandi lazım amad char tark*
> *Tark-i dunya, tark-i ukba, tark-i hasti, tark-i tark*
> *(In this way, one must renounce four things:*
> *the world, the Hereafter, "becoming," and the idea of renunciation)*[127]

This means in order to earn the pleasure of God one must first abandon the world. In *Al-Mathnawi Al-Nuri*, when Bediüzzaman describes the notion of abandoning the world, he gives the following principle: "Know, O friend, that if your intellect is sound, you should not rejoice or grieve, be angry or complain, about anything you gain or lose here, for this world is decaying, as is your own world and you."[128] This means a person who abandons the world, even if the entire world was given to him or even if he had earned a world of wealth, he would not show any joy for it. Along with showing gratitude, he would say: "O God, this wealth has no importance to me because the only thing that I care about is pleasing You." With this frame of mind, even if he loses the entire world, he will show patience thus he will not be saddened by it.

One of the best examples of abandoning the world is the situation of Prophet Ayyub. Ayyub's submission and patience should not be seen only in the endurance he had shown during his illness. It should be observed in the many tests he had being subjected to throughout his life. The Almighty God had tested him in many different ways.

One day, he saw the obliteration of his sheep by the wolves; another time he witnessed the destruction of his crops by the powerful winds. He did not show any signs of compliant as he said to his wife with total submission: "Do not worry. All of these possessions were given to me by my Lord, and now He has taken them away. Praise

[127] Nursi, Said, *The Letters*, New Jersey: The Light, 2007, p. 24
[128] Nursi, Said, *Al-Mathnawi Al-Nuri*, New Jersey: The Light, 2007, p. 185

be to the One Who has given them to me for my benefit and to the One Who has taken them away!"

On another occasion, an earthquake had taken the lives of his children. With tears of compassion flowing from his eyes, he said in total submission and patience: "Praise be to God who has entrusted these children to me and then taken them back again."

After each calamity, the devil would run to him and say, "You are a pious worshipper who devotes himself to righteousness yet God has taken your wealth and children from you! Moreover, each day your illness is becoming more severe. Are you going to continue to worship Him?" The devil did not know that his whispers of rebellion would never affect Ayyub in anyway and his efforts were in vain. Ayyub would continue to show patience to all types of disasters and calamities, he would accept everything that comes from God with pleasure as he repeated the words: "Praise be to God, Who gives and takes." Furthermore, he was in the realization of the fact that everything is a blessing from God and he was only a trustee who was relieved off his burden.

So when a person considers his worldly wealth in this regard and does not change his attitude even if he loses everything, then he has abandoned the world. Abandoning the world does not mean not earning a living or accumulating wealth. If this was the case, then encouraging the believers to form partnerships, to earn money and to become wealthy would have had no meaning. Indeed, a believer should work hard and earn lots of money but he should not do this only for his own comfort, luxury and pleasure by purchasing yachts, villas or expensive cars. A believer could become wealthy as Kharun and take pleasure out of life within the limits of what is lawful in Islam. There is no problem with this. However, the problem is when he uses his entire wealth for himself only; when he does not sacrifice from it as it becomes necessary and when he becomes spoiled and arrogant, and as a result he is squashed under the weight of his own wealth.

The second principle was *"tark-i uqba,"* abandoning the Hereafter. A person of devotion should also think about earning an eternal life in the Hereafter in return for the effort and exertion he displays on earth. However, if a person is serving, worshipping, remembering God in his recitations and Prayers or even spreading the Name of God and enduring the burdens and difficulties of this duty with a sole aim to earn and enter paradise, this person is losing on a path that normally leads to success. A devoted soul may face all of the above yet he would not use them solely for the purpose of purchasing his after-life. He should instead say: "O my Lord, if I am getting close to You by doing these things, I will regard myself as a fortunate person. I seek nothing but Your pleasure."

Yes, a devoted soul does everything to please God and endures all forms of suffering for the sake of God. This should be his sole objective hence he should show patience to everything that comes to him on this sacred path. However, he should never consider the things he does as an asset for the Hereafter or perform them so he could get something in return from God. He should always be in the mentality of "I am on the path of righteousness and I am being tested by God." Does not God say: "*We will certainly test you with something of fear and hunger, and loss of wealth and lives and fruits (earnings); but give glad tidings to the persevering and patient*" (al-Baqarah 2:155).

This means our Lord is saying to us: "I will test you with wealth, with your lives and your fears and I will show you, your own selves. That is what you are made of, how much you worth and how long you can last. You will learn about yourselves and realize when and where you may give up or lose your patience. The reason for this is, on the other side, you will decide your own fate with your own conscience.

Everything depends on our intention to earn the pleasure of God. So "abandoning the Hereafter" means one should only seek the plea-sure of God.

Another thing that should be abandoned is one's own carnal soul. *Tark-i hasti* means abandoning your ego, not thinking about yourself. For example, during the Prayer, you must to remove your physical self and abandon your ego. You should only think about Him hence you will leave your Prayer alone with Him. Every word that comes out of your mouth will signify His pleasure. In every moment of the Prayer, He shall be there. Nothing of you should intervene in any part of the

Prayer; there should be no consideration for your carnal soul. Bahauddin Naqshband defines this state as *tark-i hasti* (abandoning your existence).

After abandoning everything, one may think along the lines of "I have abandoned everything for Him, the world, the Hereafter and even myself." This is when Imam Naqshband introduces another form of abandoning: *"tark-i tark"* and claims that this is also necessary. This means one should also abandoned the things he has abandoned, in other words, one should not even remind himself about the virtuous things he has done. If one thinks to himself "I have abandoned this and that" then he has not truly abandoned anything yet.

Yes, sacrificing your feelings of material and spiritual benefits is quite important. And abstinence from these things has great rewards. When you remove these feelings from your mind, you begin to live a life of four dimensions based on abandoning. You will reach the profundity of abandoning the world; the depth of abandoning the acceptations of the Hereafter; the horizon of abandoning yourself and the custom of abandoning everything you have abandoned. Finally, by overcoming your own ego, you will find Him beyond everything you have abandoned. Without doubt, a person who is on the path to pleasing God will achieve proximity to Him depending on the amount of sacrifices he makes from his feelings of material and spiritual *fuyud*.

READING TEXT
What Have We Sacrifices for God?

I think about it and I feel I should be ashamed of myself, yet I cannot even do that. This means even the feeling of embarrassment is a sign of virtue or a quality. I ask myself:

"What have I lost for God? Have I given something of value? Did I make a sacrifice or given up on something of significance to me?"

For example, did I lose my rank or wealth? Was I discharged from my position? Did I lose my reputation? No, none of these have occurred! Yet, losing these things would not even be considered as a great sacrifice. Just as shaved bread grows thicker, our Lord will replace these things with a better and more blessed ones. Let us raised the bar as we ask the same question: "Have we lost our limbs or organs which could not be replaced?"

This is what the issue is; my hands, arms, feet, eyes and ears are all fine. I have not lost any of them on the path of God. Yet, I see people who have lost their wealth, health, rank and limbs and these people do not even complain about a thing. I cannot even think about being doleful. Let us take a look at the following example:

It was a time in history when some false Prophets had emerged. During the battle of Yamama, father Tufayl had been martyred and his son Amir lost his arm. Amir was not despaired. On the contrary, he wished he had also lied as a martyred on the hot desert sands, just as his father did.

He was thinking to himself, "I it wasn't in my destiny to become a martyr like my father."

One day he sat at the gathering of Umar as he listened to a speech. They brought some food and everyone sat down around the table yet Amir stayed away. No matter how much they insisted, he would not sit down. Umar realized why he was reluctant as he said: "You have lost your right arm and you do not wish to eat with your left hand. This is why you refrain from sitting with us!"

Then the Caliph Umar continued: "There is not a person amongst us whose arm has entered paradise before his body. It would be sad for us to sit down around a feast where you are absent. It is a great honor for us to sit down with you. Come sit with us and let us have the honor of eating with a person whose limb has gone to heaven before his body. At least this would be our consolation. Let us say: "O Lord, we have not sacrificed one of our limbs on your path, but we are sitting with a brother who did! Forgive us for his sake!"

I think about this incident a lot and I keep on saying to myself: "Forget about sacrificing your wealth, rank and possessions, these people used to sacrifice their lives and limbs. They used to send their organs to paradise before themselves. Those who were aware of this self-sacrifice and altruism considered sitting with them as an honor. Even the great Caliph Umar was asking for intercession from them.[129]

Does not this incident teach us something? Should we not derive a lesson from it?

Altruism in This Day and Age

The last century was a period in which calamities, disasters and catastrophes have rained upon our people. It would be difficult to show another era in which so many calamities piled up one after the other on a same nation or society. More than ever, the people of today need the truth, reality and the sound of Qur'anic breaths. Consequently, people who are going to undertake this task should be extremely self-sacrificing thus they should attend to the problems of our people just like a compassionate doctor and with great understanding of servanthood.

If the example is suitable, a great ship has been aground. There is a need for enormous support and self-sacrifice so the ship could set sail again. Every ideology needs support and self-sacrifice that is proportional to its greatness and value. The self-sacrifice required of the movement depends on the enormity and greatness of the ideal. That is to say, if the level of self-sacrifice is kept at the same level as the previous centuries, we will not accomplish what is expected of us. A required service can only be achieved if the level altruism is kept above the normal, just like the sacrifice made by the Companions of the Prophet.

Our faith requires the self-sacrifice from us today. Praise be to God that many incidents of altruism which reminds us of the Companions are also witnessed today, hence this gives us hope for the future. Fethullah Gülen talks about one of these incidents during his sermon: "There was a man who used to sell *lahmajun* (Turkish pita made with mince meat). He was a self-sacrificing soul who came to me about two years ago and said: "My respected teacher, you are looking for a place where students could stay. I have bought two houses by working with this pushcart stall as I sold *lahmajun* on the streets for many

---

[129] Şahin, Ahmed , *Olaylar Konuşuyor*, İstanbul: Cihan, 2001, p. 28

years. One of these houses is enough for me. If you accept, I like to give the other one for student accommodation."

I could not refuse such an offer made with an intention to please God. I hoped that by accepting, my Lord would also forgive me using his altruism as an intercession.

This person who had given his heart to God did not stop there. He was hungry for good deeds. A six or seven months later, he came back again and said: "My respected teacher, there is a big garden in front of my house, I want to build a boarding school there and accommodate one hundred students."

I looked at the face of this man who sold *lahmajun* in the streets with a small pushcart and in bafflement I asked: "How are you going to build a boarding school by selling *lahmajun* on the streets?"

He replied: "Do not worry; with your prayers and the blessing of God, I shall accomplish this."

He did what he said and by selling *lahmajun* from that small pushcart, he built a boarding school. Obviously, he had made great sacrifices from his personal life in order to save this kind money. A friend of mine had seen his shoes one day and realized that they were unwearable. He told him he needed a pair of used shoes and asked if anyone had a pair. This was a man who had sacrificed himself to the truth and given his heart to God. This is how a true altruist was supposed to be.

It is the responsibility of the people of faith to spread the truths of faith. This duty is a cause bigger and more important than any issue on earth. This is why a believer must make time to worship, serve faith, and to discipline his soul with knowledge.

Moreover, he should spend his time on guiding and inviting the new generation to a virtuous life through discipline and practice. This should be done with extreme care, interest and strength. Believers should consider the superfluous things which are seen as beauties by worldly people as meaningless hence they should not waste their time with them.

How fortunate are those who consider the life-style of the indecent people which is embellished on the outside but filthy in the inside, pretty on the outside and decomposed in the inside, as nothing but meaningless fun and games hence they do not feel any interest towards them and ruin their eternal contentment. A thousand greetings to those who sacrifice their time for building an "Age of Happiness" for future generations and for a cause that promises eternal happiness.[130]

READING TEXT

The Altruism of the Ansar Had Brought
Tears to Everyone's Eyes

The Messenger of God was sitting by himself. The door opened and the members of the Muhajirin began to walk in. It was an interesting scene because there was no one from the Ansar amongst them. One wondered why they had not invited any member of the Ansar. They asked for permission and explained their concerns:

"O Messenger of God! We migrated to this place for the sake of God. The only intention we had was to be with you on the path of God. However, our Ansar brothers are showing so much care towards us that we fear we will consume the rewards of the Hereafter on earth. Our brothers should permit us to look after ourselves from now on. We would like to give back the things they have put aside for us. We feel humiliated and obligated to them."

They were all weeping as they explained this. Upon hearing this, the noble Messenger of God could not hold his tears back either. Perhaps, this was a scene that made the entire inhabitants of the heavens weep. This was a clash of altruism and contentment. History had never witnessed such a beautiful clash.

The cause for this beautiful disagreement would become more evident when the Prophet called the Ansar a few minutes after and explained the situation to them. However, they would oppose to the proposal made by their brothers and ask the Muhajirin to reconsider their decision. For the Ansar, accepting this offer was like splitting their bodies in half, because, they had become one with their brothers hence separating from them was same as death.

---

[130] Yıldız, Vehbi, *İlim ve İrfan Nesli*, İstanbul: Işık, 2006, p. 226

Soon all the Ansar and the Muhajirin had gathered around the noble Messenger. They were all weeping. Although, they lived in the same region and came together five times a day at the Masjid an-Nabawi, separating from the rooms they shared and the dinner table they sat down on was painful.

Yes, one side represented contentment and the other altruism and munificence. The Muhajirin asked for permission and spoke: "O Messenger of God! We migrated to Medina for the sake of God. We deserted our homes and land for God. We did not think of anything but spreading the religion of God. Our Ansar brothers have done too much for us as they acted munificently with outmost generosity. We fear that we would consume the rewards of the Hereafter on earth. O Messenger of God, we could not convince our Ansar brothers; please speak to them on our behalf. Tell them to let us go. Let us find our own homes. Tell them not to bring their harvests to us and tell them not to cook for us anymore. The burden of this obligation is too much; we do not want them to think about looking after us anymore."

They were extremely emotional as they wept severely. The noble Messenger had also become quite emotional as he said to Ansar: "Your Muhajirin brothers are saying: "They took care of us with extreme sensitivity, we feel humiliated. Where is the pleasure of God, if we are going to get something in return for the things we do for Islam?"

This is how the Messenger of God had blown the essence of brotherhood into their souls; this is how he had mesmerized and amalgamated them. He had molded and shaped them like honey-wax.[131] This concept kept the Muslim society alive for centuries and protected the feelings of brotherhood and the excitement of servanthood from erosion as it also prevented Muslims from falling into conflicts over wealth, worldly gains, interests, ranks and positions.

Why Did Bediüzzaman Refused to Accept Gifts?

Bediüzzaman spent every period of his life serving the religion and society with altruism, self-sacrifice and abstinence. He never changed

---

[131] Gülen, M. Fethullah, *Sonsuz Nur-2*, İstanbul: Nil, 2007, p. 117

his stands as he constantly said: "Our duty is the duty of the Companions and in this mission there is starvation, troubles, burdens and more." He would not accept gifts from no one. If one of his beloved students brought him a bunch of grapes, he would give him a gift in return. To those who insisted, he would say: "This is my principle, do not break it for it will bother me." The *Risale-i Nur* students who were at his service had never witnessed him to accept a gift without giving something in return. People who saw this would ask: "He does not take anything from no one, how does he manage?" Of course, Bediüzzaman was benefiting from the wisdom of thrift and Divine blessings. Let us now give some examples of his abstinence from accepting gifts.

When he was at Barla, he would visit the grape farms of his friends. He would pluck two grapes from the vinery and ask: "How much is it, I would like to pay for this." People of Barla were generous hence they felt honored when Bediüzzaman ate from their fruit gardens. However, he would always pay for whatever he took. He always carried loose change in his pockets. Sometimes he would present a *Risale* as a gift for what he had eaten. If Bediüzzaman accepted gifts, he would have a number of properties in Barla.

Ceylan Çalışkan Ağabey who had been with him since he was only a boy, kept records by writing things on pieces of small paper. He had written with his hand writing that Bediüzzaman never accepted gifts without giving something in return. Moreover, he would always give something to those who supported or served him.

On one of the notes written by Ceylan Ağabey, Bediüzzaman said to him: "Ceylan! Rabia, who has been doing my laundry for the past year, has sent me a shirt and some coal for winter. I have an obligation to her for a year of laundry; therefore, I cannot return her gift. I want to be of some benefit to her, so send her the Zamzam water and the dates that arrived from Mecca and give her my regards."

Before they had purchased a motor vehicle, Bediüzzaman and his students would frequently walk through the countryside and sometimes they would come across some motorists. The drivers would stop immediately and insist: "Please let me drive you home." He would not turn them down but he always paid something for their services. He would say: "I would be breaking my own principle if I do not give something." He would also preach them by saying: "Being a driver is a public service. If you offer your obligatory Prayers, then your work will transform into worship." Sometimes as he walked by the gardens and farms, the owners would bring fruits and insisted that he take them as a gift. He would not turn them down but he always paid for them. To those who refused to take his money, he would say: "It will bother me if I do not give something for these, please do not break my principle." Even if his students wished to get something, he would pay for it and bargained for it. He would say: "Have you sold this to us for this price?" They would reply: "Yes we did."

After meeting Bediüzzaman in 1954 at Isparta, the *Risale-i Nur* students Mustafa Birlik and Ahmet Feyzi Kul took on an active role in İzmir to distribute the *Risale-i Nur*. It was during this period that Abdullah Yeğin had completed his duty as a military officer and indented to visit Bediüzzaman at Isparta.

Mustafa Birlik knew that Bediüzzaman's food plate was very old so he purchased some pots, pans, spoons and a scoop, and then gave it to Abdullah Ağabey who later came to visit Bediüzzaman. However, Bediüzzaman wrote him a letter saying: *"Keçeli*, don't you know my principles, why have you sent these?" (*"Keçeli"* is a word Said Nursi often uses when addressing his loyal students, sometimes to gently reprimand them, other times as a joke to compliment them).

Although they were not expensive things, Bediüzzaman assigned them a value of 20 liras. In the same letter he wrote: "Which book would you want? I shall send it to you." Mustafa Ağabey did not take the matter so seriously, yet sometimes later when he came to visit him again, Bediüzzaman asked: "Did you get the book that was worth 20 liras?" If Mustafa Ağabey said yes, it would have been a lie, so he said: "No, I did not." Then Bediüzzaman insisted: Which book do you want?" Mustafa Ağabey had no other alternative but to take a book which was worth 20 liras.[132]

---

[132] Duman, Murat, *Bir Fikir ve Aksiyon İnsanı Bediüzzaman Said Nursi*. İstanbul: Gelecek, 2008, pp. 78–80

The *Risale-i Nur*'s Mission Is Material
and Spiritual Altruism

Bediüzzaman lived an efficient life and never depended on anyone. Throughout his life he followed the principles of efficiency. He would eat less, sleep less and live a simple life. A loaf of bread was enough for him for a week; he would wear the same garment for a year and he did not refrain from wearing clothes that had patches all over them. Including gifts, he would never accept anything as he continued his life with certain principles and these self-imposed rules became a source of strength for him and gave him success in his ideals.

He would explain this reality with the following words: "The mission of the *Risale-i Nur* is material and spiritual altruism. I have sacrificed everything I had, both material and spiritual and I have endured all forms of calamities. I showed endurance and patience to all types of tortures. It is because of this that the truths of faith were distributed to all regions of our nation. And because of this the *Risale-i Nur* raised hundreds of thousands or perhaps millions of students. From now on, they will continue on this path, in the service of faith. They will not detach themselves from my mission of self-sacrifice and given up on everything material and spiritual. They will work only, but only, for the sake of God. I advice my students to refrain from carrying feelings of revenge in their hearts towards those who have tormented and tyrannized us and in retaliation, I would want them to work for the *Risale-i Nur* with loyalty and consistency.[133]

Bediüzzaman was quite careful about the following five essentials:

1. He invented a method of teaching which was unique to him. He would mix the modern sciences and use them to confirm some religious truths and tried to enlighten his students in this manner.

2. He would never accept gifts and salary for his services. Yes, although he never possessed any wealth and lived a life of poverty and torment, a life which took him to banishment, exile,

[133] Nursi, Said, *Emirdağ Lahikası*, İstanbul: Şahdamar, 2011

prison, various calamities and troubles, he never requested money from anyone nor did he accept gifts without given something in return.

3. He never asked any questions to any scholar. For twenty years he continuously answered questions. In relation to this, he said: "I could never deny the knowledge of the scholars. However, asking questions to them is too much. If anyone doubts my knowledge, let them ask a question and I shall answer."

4. He prohibited his close students from taking gifts and alms too. He made them work only for the sake of God. On many occasions he would provide financial support to them.

5. He never showed any interest to worldly things. He protected his desires from transitory pleasures of the world. This is why he said: "When the time comes, I should be able to carry all my belongings with one hand and go." When asked why, he replied: "A day will come when everyone will envy my situation. Moreover, wealth and affluence does not provide any pleasure for me. I consider this world as a guest house."[134]

READING TEXT

Would a Caliph Be a Street Porter?

One night as Umar walked around the streets of the city, he heard the cries of a woman whose children had not eaten for two days.

"May God hold Umar responsible for this!" As Umar heard this he began to tremble in front of their door. Then he shouted through the door: "What do you want from Umar?"

"Why do you ask? Are you a friend or a foe?" she replied.

"I ask in the Name of God, as a friend," Umar said.

"What I want from Umar is this: He sent the father of these children to the military. My children have been starving for two days. I placed a pot of hot water on the fire and I am pretending to cook

---

[134] Nursi, Said, *Tarihçe-i Hayat*, İstanbul: Şahdamar, 2011

something for them. Yesterday, it worked and I put them to sleep but tonight they feel so hungry that they refuse to go to bed. They are moaning."

"Have you notified Umar about this?" asked Umar.

"What should I tell him? Just as he takes our men to the army, he should also think about their families. Does being a leader mean being a nuisance?" she said.

Quickly, Umar ran to his house with tears in his eyes. With a bag of flour on his back and a bowl of oil in his hand, he began to walk towards the woman's house. On the way, a Companion saw Umar and said: "O leader of the believers! Where are you going with these things? Let me carry them for you."

"I cannot give these to you; they are the sins of Umar! You may carry my load today but you cannot carry my sins on the Day of Judgment! So, let me carry them," said Umar.

Then Umar entered the house and took some flour from the bag and placed it into a pot. A part of his beard caught fire as he tried to blow into the fire that was about to go out. Then he cooked a flour soup for the children and fed them. He said to the mother: "Tomorrow, you must go and see the Caliph!"

The woman was extremely pleased about the kindness of this man as she did not know who he was. She said: "May God make you our leader, instead of Umar!"

Umar walked away without saying anything. The next morning, she went to the quarters of the Caliph and saw that the man who cooked dinner for her children was sitting in the chair of the Caliph. She realized her mistake and said: "Forgive me O Umar! Last night I was so hurt and I said things that I should not have and thus I broke your heart."

Umar replied: "No, Umar is at fault! You did what you had to do. It is you who should forgive me!"

This is how they were…

QUESTIONS

1. A phrase that describes the notion of "no one could feel the same pain or sadness of some who actually suffers the pain" is: "Fire burns where it falls." How does an altruist believer reply to this?

   a. Fire does not only burn where it falls, but it also burns its surroundings.

   b. No matter where a fire falls, it will first burn me.

   c. Fire will fall to a place and then spread to surrounding areas and then it will burn me too.

   d. Fire burns where it falls. Others will never understand this.

2. Which of the words below are close in meanings?

   a. Brotherhood – Zeal

   b. Modesty – Loneliness

   c. Altruism – Self-sacrifice

   d. Loyalty – Chastity

3. A human being should be a prosecutor for his own faults, but a .... for the faults of others.

   a. a court clerk

   b. a lawyer

   c. worker

   d. an actor

4. Which term describes the meaning of a higher level of generosity which is defined as thinking of others before yourself and caring for their interests before your own:

   a. altruism

   b. courage

   c. piety

   d. egotism

5. "A person who only thinks of himself is either not a human being or he is an incomplete human being." Who made this statement:

   a. Sayyid Qutb

   b. Bediüzzaman Said Nursi

    c. Necip Fazıl Kısakürek

    d. M. Fethullah Gülen

6. Which of the below statements is incorrect?

    a. A lover of truth who makes altruism a part of his nature will always be sensitive towards what goes around him.

    b. An altruist is a careless and neglectful person.

    c. Altruism is not a behavior restricted to human beings.

    d. Before anything, a believer displays his altruism when he fulfils his servanthood.

7. Which of the below words is related to the following concept: "sacrificing one's own interests, material and spiritual gains and even his pride and honor for the sake of a greater cause"

    a. Nationalism

    b. Benevolence

    c. Ostentation

    d. Licentiousness

8. Which of the below cannot be a quality of an altruist?

    a. Every sacrifice he makes revolves around sincerity.

    b. He does not expect material or spiritual support from people; he does everything for the sake of God.

    c. He does not leave the society he helps, under obligation.

    d. He can refrain from altruism if there is a risk of poverty.

9. Abstinence or abandoning is a fundamental essential of the Naqshbandi Order. Muhammad Bahauddin Naqshband encourages his followers to abandon four things. Which of the below is not one of these four things:

    a. The Qur'an

    b. The Hereafter

    c. Ego

    d. World

10. When the verse: *"You will never be able to attain godliness and virtue until you spend of what you love (in God's cause, or to provide sustenance for the needy). Whatever you spend, God has full knowledge of it"* was revealed, which Companion of the Proph-

Qualities of a Devoted Soul

et wanted to donate his garden of Bayruha which was located across the Masjid an-Nabawi?

a. Abu Talib
b. Abu Bakr
c. Abu Talha
d. Abu Amr

6

CONSULTATION (*ISTISHARAH*)

Ask someone who knows. The knowledge of two is more blessed than one. (Proverb)

What is Consultation?

Consultation means to exchange ideas on a certain topic to reach the truth. In the Qur'an, God says: *"Then pardon them, pray for their forgiveness, and take counsel with them in the affairs..."* (Al Imran 3:159) and *"...whose affairs are by consultation among themselves..."* (ash-Shura 42:38).

Therefore, with these verses, God signifies the importance of consultation and the fact that it is an important principle for the believers.

Referring to Umar and Abu Bakr, the noble Messenger of God once said: "I will not act in opposition to you if you two agree upon something through consultation."[135] Our noble Prophet who said, "Those who consult will never feel regret"[136] have encouraged his followers to act through consultation and he too requested the views of the Ansar when he heard the news of Abu Sufyan arriving to Badr. Moreover, he consulted his Companions in many issues such as about the situation of prisoners at Badr, prior to the battles of Uhud and al-Khandaq (the Trench), during the *ifq* incident at Hudaybiyah and in regards to the calling of the *adhan*.[137]

---

[135] Ahmad ibn Hanbal, *Al-Musnad*, 5/227
[136] Heysemi, Nuruddin, *Macmau'z-Zawaid*, 2/280
[137] Ibn Sa'd, *At-Tabakat*, 2/350–352

In another *hadith*, our noble Prophet said: "A nation will never fall into dissension for as long as they adhere to consultation."[138] With this *hadith* he indicates to the fact that a person may make an error in judgment but the views of a consultation committee will be accurate.

One must value consultation as a commandment from God and as a Sunnah of His noble Messenger. Our ancestors said: "Those who listen to greats minds will conquer great mountains." And by suggesting that some intellects are higher than others, they explained the significance of consultation with a short summary.

Consultation Is the Commandment of the Qur'an

Luqman Hekim says: "Before doing something, consult someone who has done it before, because, he will give his opinion to you for free on matters that may have cost him dearly." No matter how smart a person is, he is on the wrong path unless he consults others in relation to solving issues. Even our noble Prophet, who was the smartest of all human beings, solved issues through consultation. There are many examples of this during the Age of Happiness:

During the battle of Badr, our noble Prophet wanted to camp near the closest water wells. Al-Hubab ibn al-Mundhir came to him and said: "O Messenger of God! Did you choose this place because God has commanded it hence we are not permitted to go any further? Or is it just a part of your battle strategy?"

"No, it is just an opinion, a battle strategy," replied the noble Prophet.

"O Messenger of God, then this is not a good place to camp! We should go to the wells that are closest to the enemy. Then, we should make a small pool there and destroy the other wells so that the enemy does not benefit from them."

The Messenger of God replied: "This is a good idea." Then he did what the Companion suggested.[139]

---

[138] Zamakhshari, *Al-Kashshaf*, 1/332
[139] Ibn Hisham, *As-Sirah*, 2/277

Yes, consultation is the commandment of the Qur'an and thus it is a form of worship. Those who have chosen the truths of the Qur'an as a guide to themselves must obey its commandments and deal with their issues through consultation.

Consultation also means that human beings need each other. In other words, they are a group of people who love, respect and need each other; therefore, they value each other's opinion and they accept the notion of consultation as a fundamental principle amongst themselves and hence act accordingly.

A person, who does not consult with people of experience, does not love his colleagues. Moreover, it means he does not value the views of others because he believes his opinion is always better than the opinion of others.

Since we cannot think of a person who does not need anyone, a person who refrains from consultation is an individual who is oblivious of his own nature which is based on impotence, deficiency and destitution. Such attitude is quite dangerous for a human being. Giving importance to consultation does not come from deficiency but it originates from maturity and the thought of doing a better service.[140]

We Should Not Do Anything without Consultation

"Those who consult with others will not be deprived of reaching the truth."[141] These are the words of Imam al-Ghazali. We should always adhere to consultation so that we do not feel regret afterwards. A believer should always act through consultation whether it is their personal business or an issue that concerns his friends whom he shares the same path.

A decision made by a single mind will not have the same accuracy as a decision made by ten minds. Accordingly, no job should be done without consultation. Those who act without consultation are following their own personal thoughts. It is easier for such people to make mistakes. As a fundamental principle, before using his own views and

---

[140] Yıldız, Vehbi, *İlim ve İrfan Nesli*, İstanbul: Işık, 2006, p. 231
[141] Al-Ghazali, *Ihya*, 2/98

experiences, a believer should always give importance to consultation and to the views of a collective consensus.

The fact that although our noble Prophet received Divine revelations and still consulted his Companions on certain matters, teaches us the Prophet's views on the importance of consensus.

Our noble Prophet would share his views with the entire community by sometimes consulting with opinion leaders one by one and on other occasions by gathering all of them to discuss an issue or to solve a problem.

It is a fact that a decision made by consensus is binding to each member in the meeting, thus everyone who has the authority to vote is responsible. Since those who give their opinions in the matter at hand will feel responsible and do their best to solve the issue, therefore the decision will be more accurate and guaranteed. The feeling of responsibility is an essential of an individual character therefore the principle of consultation has a disciplinary feature.[142]

By using the power of consultation, our noble Prophet encouraged everyone to own up to an issue. This is an important factor in human productivity. As a matter of fact, people feel honored when their opinions are valued hence take on responsibility in regards to the matter at hand. Consequently, consultation has a positive impact on productivity.

READING TEXT

Prophet Sulayman's Consultation with Hudhud

Sulayman is a great Prophet who has been blessed with a kingdom both on earth and in the Hereafter. One day, an angel came to Prophet Sulayman with a glass of water in his hand and said: "O the sultan of humans and other creatures! This glass of water I hold in my hand is called "the water of life." If you drink this you will have a long life, thus you will live for many centuries. Many tribes will perish and be replaced by new ones but your sovereignty will continue. All you have to do is drink this water!"

---

[142] Canan, İbrahim, *Peygamberimizin Tebliğ Metotları*, İstanbul: Nesil, 2002, p. 339

Prophet Sulayman thought for a little while and then he replied: "Let me gather my birds and consult them, I will tell you my decision after."

One day, when all of his birds were gathered at the desert, he asked: "An angel offered me the water of life and said that if I drank it, I would live for many centuries and rule my kingdom. What do you say, should I drink it?"

All the birds replied: "Drink it O master so you could live for a long time!"

However, the Hudhud bird was not amongst them hence he could not get its opinion. Upon the conclusion of the consultation, Hudhud flew in and landed amongst the other birds. Prophet Sulayman noticed this and said: "One of your brothers was not at the meeting so we should also ask his opinion. Perhaps he may have a different perspective which may broaden our horizon."

Prophet Sulayman explained the situation to Hudhud and requested his opinion. Hudhud replied: "Do not drink the water of life master!"

"Can you tell me why," asked Prophet Sulayman.

"Isn't it obvious sire? When you drink this water, you will live for many centuries hence all your friends and brothers would have died then. As they taste death one by one, you will feel their pain and anguish. Then you will make new friends and companions. But they will too die and leave you behind. Again you will suffer with their separation. What kind of life is this that will give you nothing but suffering and anguish by continuously taking your loved ones away from you?" said Hudhud.

Prophet Sulayman thought for awhile and then asked all the birds who were there: "Why do you say about your brother Hudhud's views?"

"We agree with our brother, Hudhud's opinion is more accurate than ours. We suggest that you change your decision on this matter," they said.

Prophet Sulayman summoned the angel who brought the water of life and said: "I have decided not to drink the water of life! I think that it is more blessed to die just as everyone else. Whether one lives a long life or a short one, he still dies at the end. Take this water of life away. A limited life is enough for me."[143]

The Prisoners of Badr Were Released after Consultation

The battle of Badr was managed through consultation right from the beginning to the end. The battle had ended with a victory to Muslims and there were many prisoners. This was a new situation Muslims had not dealt with before. This was the first war they had encountered hence they had never dealt with the issue of prisoners before and there were no written rules of engagement. Moreover, a Divine revelation in relation to this issue was not revealed yet. They could not just let the prisoners go because they would have rejoined their army and come back to fight them again. This in turn would mean giving the idol worshippers another chance to gather their army.

For this reason, our noble Prophet gathered his Companions and began to consult them about the situation of the prisoners. This was a first and a step taken now would be a method to follow in the future.

The Messenger of God asked: "What do you think we should do about the prisoners? Although most of them were your brothers before, now God has left it up to you to decide their fate!"

Abu Bakr replied first: "O Messenger of God! Even though God has granted you victory over them, they are still your relatives and people! Some of these people are our cousins, some are from the same origin and some are brothers! The best option would be to get a ransom for them and then release them. The ransom we get for their release will strengthen our hand towards disbelief. Perhaps, because of this, God will soften their hearts and one day they might come and support you!"

After listening to the views of his loyal Companion, the noble Prophet turned to Umar and said: "O the son of Khattab! What do you say about this?"

"O Messenger of God! These people banished you from your land. They declared you as a liar and they came to kill you! They fought

---

[143] Şahin, Ahmet, *Dini Hikayeler*, İstanbul: Cihan, 2009, p. 92

with you. I do not think along the same lines as Abu Bakr. Give them to me and I shall execute them. I do not want these people to be prisoners in your hand," Umar said.

The consultation continued but a general view was beginning to form. The opinion of the Prophet was also to release them. All the verses which were revealed to date were talking about forgiveness and inviting people to religion with kind and wise words. He was a soul who had become one with the Qur'an and forgiveness was part of his character. For this reason he agreed with the majority and decided to release the prisoners with ransom.

There were further flexibilities where people who could not find the required amount would be given a concession. However, there were also those who had nothing and the Prophet wished that they could be freed as well. Finally, they found a solution for this as well. Those who had no money would be released upon teaching ten young Muslim men how to write and read.

Yet there were also some prisoners who had no money and did not know how to write or read. They would also be saved from this difficulty. All they had to do was to give their words that they would never speak against Islam and aid those who were against it and they would be released.[144]

Interestingly, prior to the battle of Uhud two different opinions emerged from the consultation. According to one view, it would be better to remain in Medina and defend the city. The other view suggested that the battle be fought outside of Medina. The view of the Prophet was to defend the city yet he went along with the views of the majority.

There was a consultation gathering prior to the Battle of the Trench also. During this consultation, Salman al-Farisi had suggested a trench be built around the city and the Prophet accepted his proposal.

The noble Prophet gave great importance to consultation and chose to consult his Companions in every issue which was not covered by revelation. His method helped the Companions become part of the solution more easily and promptly. On the other hand, it is a

---

[144] Ibn Hisham, *As-Sirah*, 3/211

known fact that those who are not part of the solution are part of the problem. Accordingly, with great skills, our noble Prophet has shown us the importance of consultation by consulting his Companions and making them a part of the solution. In this sense, he has used their energy in a most productive way.[145]

READING TEXT

If You Have Intelligence, Become a Friend
with another Intellect

Rumi says: "If you have intelligence, become friends with another intellect and seek his advice." Abbasid ruler Al-Ma'mun who made this saying a principle for himself gave the following advice to his son: "When in doubt, seek the advice of experienced, zealous, compassionate old men. This is because; they have seen many things and witnessed the ups and downs of time and the success and downfalls of the past. Even if their words are painful, endure and embrace them. Do not invite those who are coward, liars, greedy, arrogant and obstinate to your consultation committee."

Arrogant people will never value the opinions of others hence they will not consult others. They will try to solve their issues through their own personal views. Such behavior would most of the time result in failure. Therefore, instead of benefits, it will bring harm.

One should never forget the word *istisharah* means to collect honey from the bee. Honey means remedy. Consequently, *istisharah* (consultation) will provide remedy for problems at an individual, family and community level. The entire history is the biggest witness to reality.

Those Who Request the Opinion of Others Are More Successful than a Genius

Consultation is a method that minimizes mistakes and prevents making wrong decisions on an issue. Thoughts such as "I can make my

---

[145] Yenibaş, Hasan, "Peygamberimiz'in İnsan Unsurunu Verimli Kullanması," *Yeni Ümit*, issue 82, p. 27

own decisions, I do not need to consult others" will take people to the losing streak. The reason for this is an intellect is higher than another intellect. In the words of Fethullah Gülen, "A decision made on a matter without deep contemplation, and without presenting it to the views and critics of others will most of the time result in failure and disappointment. Even if he is a genius, a person closed to other opinions, hence do not respect the views of others, will make more mistakes than those who elect to offer his views to the committee of consultation.

The most intelligent person is an individual who benefits from the views of others and respects consultation. On the other hand, those immature souls who limit themselves to their own ideas and moreover try to impose them on others will always draw the hatred of others.

Before commencing a project, we should take the necessary steps to consult others and make no mistakes in the precautionary measures so that later on we do not accuse others and destiny by doubling the effects of the calamity. If one does not think of the consequences in fine detail and does not consult those who possess experience, prior to taking on a venture, it will inevitably result in disappointment and regret.

There are many 'know-it-all people' who took on a passion without consulting anyone that the cobras they awakened had bitten them and put them out of commission. If only it was them who were put out of commission!"[146]

For Fethullah Gülen, consultation and collective consciousness are imperative principles of any positive movement. Such person evaluates the notion of collective consciousness as the common intellect of people of the service and the ideals of individuals who think of others before themselves; people who walk with hope, loyalty, sincerity and genuineness; people who have become one with the present and future of the society by thinking about the interests of society before their own benefits; people who have chosen humility, modesty and self-criticism over fame.[147]

---

[146] Gülen, M. Fethullah, *Ölçü veya Yoldaki Işıklar*, İstanbul: Nil, 2011, pp. 171–172
[147] See Gülen, M. Fethullah, *Yeşeren Düşünceler*, İstanbul: Nil, 2011, pp. 108–114

Who Do We Consult and What Do We Consult with Others?

One of the most important issues of consultation is, knowing whose advice we should seek. This matter has an important impact on the result of the project being a blessed one. For this reason we need to make sure that the person we ask for advice is intelligent, experienced, pious, virtuous, sincere, possesses solid views, wise and that he has the qualities of analyzing the human psychology and also the virtues of trustworthiness and honesty. On the other hand, seeking the advice of those who are ignorant, impolite and arrogant will bring no benefit to anyone.

One should not be surprised at people who always make accurate decisions when they consult others before taking on a task. The reason for this is such people test their own intellects and comprehension and by doing so they keep their minds and thoughts fresh.

Problems should be solved with one of the following two methods when consultation becomes necessary:

1. A few people can be consulted separately for advice and the point where the views join should be implemented.
2. A few people should come together where everyone could offer their own opinions on the issue. Later, these people can analyze each other's views and choose the most appropriate solution. This is a healthier version of consultation.

Why Is Consultation Necessary in Regard to Decisions That Concern the Entire Society?

The scholars of the Qur'an exegesis have answered this question under three main headers that they have derived from the Holy Qur'an and the *hadith*:

1. Consultation is necessary because if an issue concerns more than two people, a group or a community then it would be unjust for one individual to make a decision on a matter that concerns others. The accuracy of a decision made by one person is always questionable.

2. If a person wishes to make a decision on an issue that concerns the entire community, it would mean that this person is either thinking about his own interests or he ranks himself higher than others. One should understand that both alternatives are incorrect.

3. Making a decision on issues that concern two or more people is a great responsibility. A person who believes he will be held accountable in the Hereafter should refrain from making such decision alone.

Our noble Prophet and his Companions have always solved their issues through consultation. For example, as soon as Umar ibn Khattab became the Caliph, he established governmental institutes of consultation. Individuals whom the people respected were invited to these consultation committees. For example, renowned personalities from the Muhajirin and the Ansar were the members of these committees. Amongst them there were perpetual members like Uthman, Ali, Abdurrahman ibn Awf, Muadh ibn Jabal, Zaid ibn Thabit and Ubayy ibn Ka'b. This committee would come together once a week and discuss governmental and social issues and produce effective solutions. Everyone in this consultation committee proposed their views clearly and openly. The statement "You cannot have a caliphate without consultation" belongs to Umar ibn Khattab.

Uthman and Ali also gave great importance to consultation as they addressed their chief issues through consultation. The people of opinion and judgment would offer their views in comfort and with ease. Once everyone gave their opinion, they would follow the views of the majority. The decisions made by the committee in regard to general matters were legally binding.

READING TEXT

Some Important Principles of Consultation

If our views are accepted by the consultation committee, we should feel pleased; however, if they are rejected, we should say, "it is not the right time yet" hence we should never argue or go into disputes.

Sometimes, even a logical opinion may be turned down due to the person who offers it. In such situations, one should let someone else make the offer. What is important is the general acceptation of the views and opinions.

Bediüzzaman found that the services rendered in Isparta with a small number of people surpassed the services rendered in İstanbul with a large number of people. He related this success to sincerity.[148]

In a committee of consultation, one should offer his views in a most beautiful way and if they are not accepted, one should not insist.

Moreover, if the decisions made during the meeting are not clear, one should request an explanation before the meeting is over, so that he does not criticize the decision after the meeting concludes. The decision of the committee should never be criticized afterwards. The decision made by the committee is binding to those who were not there, even to those who previously opposed this view. Therefore, everyone should abide by them. The person who is on the side of the view that is supported by a minority of voters should accept the end result since he came to the consultation in the comprehension of "the committee will make the right decision."

QUESTIONS

1- Which of the below is not an example of our Prophet's views on the importance of consultation?
   a. His consultation with the Companions in regard to the prisoners of Badr
   b. His consultation about battle strategy prior to the battles of Uhud and the Trench
   c. His consultation with his wife Umm Salama at Hudaybiyah
   d. His migration from Mecca to Medina after the permission of God

2- "If you have intelligence, become friends with another intellect and seek his advice." Who made the above statement?
   a. Bediüzzaman Said Nursi
   b. Mehmet Akif Ersoy

---

[148] M. Fethullah Gülen, *Fasıldan Fasıla*, 1/89

    c. Mawlana Jalaluddin Rumi

    d. Elmalılı Hamdi Yazır

3- Which of the below is not a quality of a person whom one should consult with?

    a. Intelligent and experienced

    b. Religious and virtuous

    c. Trustworthy and honest

    d. Indecent and arrogant

4- "Ask someone who knows, the knowledge of two is better than one" What is the main theme of this statement?

    a. Altruism

    b. Genuineness

    c. Consultation

    d. Truthfulness

5- Which Companion suggested to our noble Prophet that they should camp near the closest water well to the enemy at Badr?

    a. Al-Hubab ibn al-Mundhir

    b. Mus'ab ibn Umayr

    c. Umar ibn Khattab

    d. Abu Bakr

6- Which of the below describes the situation of a person who wishes to make a decision on behalf of the community and without consulting anyone?

    a. He is only thinking about his own interests and he sees his views above everyone.

    b. The issue at hand is quite confusing and difficult to solve.

    c. It is impossible to make a decision on difficult issues through consultation.

    d. This person is thinking of the society more than himself.

7- Which of the below is a synonym of "consultation?"

    a. Collective

    b. Meeting to achieve consensus

    c. Nobility

    d. Participation

7

LOVE, PASSION, AND RENEWING ONE'S SELF

Love and Passion

One of the most imperative qualities of a person of service is running with love and passion without falling into monotony and tediousness and renewing oneself by being energetic. A member of the service should always rejuvenate and revitalize himself (herself) by commencing a new revival in his spiritual realm. The reason for this is "keeping oneself dynamic requires consistency."

This self-renewal should become a second nature to a believer; it should be a part of his natural disposition hence he should constantly deepen his faith and strengthen it through active role that revolves around service. In the Qur'an, God Almighty has informed Muslims to encourage each other to serve religion without assigning any limits to love and passion.[149]

In relation to preserving vitality with love and passion, our noble Prophet advises Abu Dharr:

"Control and renew your ship one more time because the ocean is deep. Make sure you take sufficient rations, without doubt, the journey is long. Your load should be light because the hills which you shall climb are steep. Be sincere in your deeds because our Lord, Who is All-Seeing and All-Hearing, knows about everything you do."

In the person of Abu Dharr, our noble Prophet teaches us the following lesson: If you become satisfied with the level faith you initially

---

[149] See Nisa 4:84

embraced, time and incidents will bring such things before you that your faith will wear out and erode hence you will eventually come to a breaking point. In this long journey, you should always renew and restore your ship so that you could reach the shores of salvation. On the other hand, if your ship is not strong and reliable in this world of ocean amid different types of dangerous waves and as you face various enemies such as the devil, the carnal soul and some people who represent them, it will smash into something, and as a result it will capsize and perhaps sink. For this reason, you should constantly renew yourself.

Hubayb's Love and Passion for Service Brings Tears to Our Eyes

Our noble Prophet expected service from his Companions no matter what conditions they were in. They were doing exactly that and using every opportunity by trying to enter the hearts of people without losing their love and passion for service. Here is an example:

Hubayb, who was assigned to the duty of teaching the universal virtues by the Prophet was captured by the idol worshippers and taken to Mecca. After he was kept in a dungeon for many days, he was taken out to be executed. These were the dark days of Mecca. He was sad and depressed because he felt that he could not find the opportunity to fulfill the duty of invitation to a virtuous life which was assigned to him by the Prophet. Now his hands were tied and his mouth was gagged as he walked towards the rope.

He kept on looking around to see if there was someone he could convey the message of God. However, he could not see anyone who would listen. There were however, some future Companions amongst the group. Unfortunately, their hearts had not opened to virtues yet.

Hubayb performed two units of *salah* and then said: "I would have performed my *salah* longer had I not thought that you would think I am afraid of dying." Then the rope was placed around his neck. His last moments had arrived. He was looking around desperately, but not for someone who could save him. He was searching for someone who he could save in the eternal life. Suddenly, an opportunity he never expected came his way. One of the chieftains of Mecca asked him a question.

On the surface, the question had no importance but he would use it to teach them a lesson. A spark he ignited there could have started a fire of faith in the hearts of some of the people who were present. The question was: "O Hubayb! In order to save yourself, would you have preferred that it was Muhammad who was being executed in your place now?"

Obviously, one should not ask such a question to a Muslim, especially to someone like Hubayb. However, he wanted to take this opportunity and make the most of it. He was extremely excited as he needed to say something between the emotions of joy and sorrow. He also knew that the answer had to be short just like the last *salah* he offered. He had to fit his entire life in a single sentence. He needed to speak in such way that the entire history had to stop and listen to him. It was a time when he had to make his last statement and do it in a way that he could teach them a lesson. Finally, he replied: "By God no! Have you seen a sign of betrayal on me? Executing him in my place to safe my own life aside, I would rather be executed even to protect him from a thorn piercing his noble foot."[150]

Upon saying these, he must have felt relieved from the burden of not being able to convey any message to them. He felt light as a feather. There was one last thing he had to do and that was to say goodbye to the Messenger of God and then he would walked towards Paradise. He did not even think if a goodbye message would travel from Mecca to Medina. Yet, he knew the person on the receiving end was the noble Messenger of God.

His last words were: "*Assalamu alayka ya Rasullalah!*" The noble Messenger was sitting with his Companions at Medina. Suddenly, he stood up and shouted: "*Wa alayka's-salam*, O Hubayb!"[151]

Yes, every person of the service should catch the horizon of Hubayb in the love and passion of *tabligh* so that they could be worthy of being the inheritors of the earth.[152]

---

[150] Ibn Kathir, *Al-Bidaya wa'n-nihaya*, 4/65; Ibn Hisham, *As-Sirah*, 3/181
[151] Ibn Kathir, *Al-Bidaya wa'n-nihaya*, 4/66–69
[152] Gülen, M. Fethullah, *İrşad Ekseni*, İzmir: Nil, 2001, p. 202

READING TEXT
"Self Renewal Is the Most Important
Essential of Continual Existence"

Self renewal is a concept that has a significant place in Gülen's thoughts and actions. He considers self renewal as the most important essential of continual existence. According to him, those who do not renew themselves when the time comes will soon or later wear out even if they are strong or powerful. Everything stays alive by renewing themselves. Once the process of self renewal stops, they are left to decompose just like a body without a soul.

Fethullah Gülen says that self renewal should not be confused with passion for fashion. They are two different things: Fashion is the process of make up and cover for masses that have been damaged all over, a surgery to cover up all the cracks. The other one is the real renewal where the society attains immortality through the "fountain of youth" brought from the tap of the *Khidir*, therefore it consists of action.

True renewal is reaching a climate of pure thoughts through the process of protecting the purity of the roots and the seeds and all the values that were filtered through heritage and synthesizing them with current thoughts and the mist of knowledge. Otherwise, defining modernization as a vest, a dress or a jelled hair style would be nothing but self-deceit and portraying it in such manner is nothing but an illusion or a magic trick.

An authentic renewal is appreciating and utilizing the development of sciences and the latest advantages offered by technology; holding the magnifying glass to our hearts to revise our intentions, views and opinions on regular basis; each passing day, adding something new to the honeycomb of knowledge in our hearts and every instant encouraging our minds to make an effort by filtering the entire universe through the prism of the soul.[153]

---

[153] *Sızıntı*, April 1982, issue 39, pp. 1–2

PERSEVERANCE AND DETERMINATION

L iterally, perseverance means being persistent, diligent, strong-minded, patient and having willpower. Perseverance is one of the most important qualities of the Prophets and the beloved servants of God. A believer, whose only objective is to please God, should continue on his path with perseverance and determination.

Perseverance and determination are nourished from faith. A believer who has submitted to the will of God and His density will never be discouraged by problems and calamities hence he will never lose his determination to struggle. Since he knows that all power and strength belongs to God, he will use all opportunities appear before him and compete in performing good deeds with determination and perseverance. No difficulty could deter him from fulfilling the commandments of God.

So the believers are those who show perseverance and determination to earn the pleasure of God until their last breaths. The following verse describes this clearly:

> Among the believers are men (of highest valor) who have been true to their covenant with God: among them are those who have fulfilled their vow (by remaining steadfast until death), and those who are awaiting (its fulfillment). They have never altered in any way. (al-Ahzab 33:23)

Yes amongst the believers there are those brave souls who keep their word to God. Some have fulfilled their covenant by giving their lives and others look for martyrdom.

Perseverance and determination means being consistent on the struggle without losing hope and facing all forms of difficulties with patience to achieve success. It is being in the mind frame of "With the permission of God, I can do this!" In any case, is it not determination and perseverance that act as a potion which takes human beings to success?

The Mind-boggling Perseverance and Determination of Prophet Noah

From Noah to Abraham and from Moses to Muhammad, peace be upon them, all Prophets have fulfilled their missions with great perseverance and determination. The determination they have shown in this regard is a great example to us.

For example, Noah is the first man after Adam to be given the mission of Prophethood.[154] After Adam, humanity had forgotten their true Lord and began to worship the stars. They had built idols to represent the stars in the heavens and gave them the names of the stars. When Noah was given the mission of Prophethood, he explained to them they were on the wrong path, and they should be worshipping God and if they embraced the faith their sins would be forgiven by God.[155] With great perseverance and determination, Noah explained the truths and his Lord to his tribe for 950 years[156], yet on each occasion, his tribe ridiculed and tried to silence him.[157] Finally, he lost hope. Then he asked his Lord to make a judgment between him and his tribe as he prayed for the salvation of a handful of people who believed him.[158] He continued his prayer with the following words: *"My Lord, I have surely called my people night and day, but my call has only caused them to flee more and more (from accepting the truth). Every time I have called them so that You may forgive them, they have thrust their*

---

[154] *Sahih al-Bukhari*, Anbiya, 3
[155] Nuh 71:2–4
[156] Al-Ankabut 29:4
[157] Nuh 71:7
[158] Ash-Shuara 26:117–118

fingers in their ears, and wrapped themselves up in their garments, and grown obstinate and more and more arrogant (in refusing my call)."[159]

"Noah (turned to his Lord, and) said: 'My Lord! They have disobeyed me and followed those whose wealth and children have increased them only in loss and self-ruin. They have made tremendous schemes (to prevent my call and people's acceptance of it).' They have said: 'Do not ever abandon your deities; do not abandon (in particular) Wadd, nor Suwa, nor Yaghuth, and Yauq, and Nasr!' They have indeed led many astray. And (O God,) increase not these wrongdoers in anything but further straying (by way of just punishment for all that they have done)."[160]

The Almighty God accepted the prayer of Noah and through Gabriel, He instructed Noah to build an Ark.[161] Prophet Noah commenced the construction of the Ark immediately after receiving the instructions of angel Gabriel. Finally, the Ark was built and all believers were ready to board as they waited for God's permission. As the sign came, Prophet Noah took only the believers on board and a pair of each animal and then left. Those who remained were destroyed.[162]

In relation to the topic, we can also use the examples of Prophet Abraham's perseverance even at a point when he was being cast into a blazing inferno, Prophet Moses and his determination and courage against the pharaoh and the patience of Prophet Ayyub with the illness which he suffered for many years.

Our Noble Prophet Was Explaining Islam contrary to All the Difficulties He Faced

One of the most important reasons behind our Prophet's success is the determination, patience and perseverance he displayed in the course of his mission. Throughout his life, our noble Prophet faced many obstacles yet he continued towards his objectives with great perseverance and determination.

---

[159] Nuh 71:5–7
[160] Nuh 71:21–24
[161] Hud 11:36–37
[162] Hud 11:40

In order to become a true believer, it is not enough to reach the peak of faith only. At the same time it is imperative that as one walks in the name of faith, he should also show the necessary resistance when he comes across obstacles and barriers. For this reason, the Holy Qur'an provides many examples from the previous Prophets and the difficulties they had faced in regard to their people so that the followers of Prophet Muhammad, peace and blessings be upon him, could prepare themselves for the possible problems that may arise in the future.

In the Qur'an, God informs us:

> Alif. Lam. Mim. Do people reckon that they will be left (to themselves at ease) on their mere saying, "We believe," and will not be put to a test? We certainly tested those who preceded them. (This is Our unchanging way) so that God will certainly mark out those who prove true (in their profession of faith), and He will certainly mark out those who prove false. (al-Ankabut 29:1–3)

This means declaring, "We believe" is not enough to face the unexpected problems of the future. Obviously, faith is the most important thing but facing all forms of difficulties with great determination and perseverance for the sake of faith is also important. In the Hereafter, great bounties await the believers. However, to achieve this, we need to show great effort and determination. Since this world is not a place of rewards, the fruits of the work we do here will mostly be harvested in the Hereafter and hence difficulties will be faced and lived here. As hell is not unnecessary, paradise is not cheap. In order to reach such a blessing, a believer must exhibit his persistency by standing firm against all the odds.

In relation to the above, our Lord says:

> (Given the history of humankind in this world,) do you think that you will enter Paradise while there has not yet come upon you the like of what came upon those who passed away before you? They were visited by such adversities and hardships, and were so shaken as by earthquake that the Messenger and those who believed in his company nearly cried out: "When comes God's help?" Beware! The help of God is surely near! (al-Baqarah 2:214)

The chieftains of Quraysh came to the door of Abu Talib to express their feelings of apprehension in relation to the efforts of the believers which increased each passing day: "Listen, O Abu Talib! Without doubt, you are the most experienced elderly person amongst us. And in relation to your status, you rank higher than all of us. We came to you before and requested that you to put a stop to your nephew's activities. Yet you did nothing about it. By God, our patience has run out as he continues to insult our idols, accuses our leaders with corruption and denounces our ancestors. When will you put a stop to this! If you like, release him from your protection so that we could solve our problem between us until one party is destroyed."

Abu Talib was constantly being pressured by these rogue disbelievers. Finally, he called his nephew and said: "O the son of my Brother! Think about me and yourself. Do not load unbearable weight on me!"[163]

Upon hearing the words of his uncle, the noble Messenger assumed for a moment that his uncle had given up and that he would not protect him anymore. However, he informed his uncle that no matter what happens, he would never give up: "My dear uncle! By God, in order to change my mind, even if they placed the sun in one of my hands and the moon in other, I will not be discouraged and I will continue on this path until God grants me victory!"[164]

They Had Placed the Intestines of a Camel on His Head

It is an interesting manifestation of destiny that most of his archenemies were his neighbors. Abu Lahab's house was right next to the Prophet's house. His other neighbors were Hakam ibn Abi'l-As, Uqba ibn Abu Muayt, Adiyy ibn Hamrah and Ibnu'l-Asda al-Hudali. Their enmity was no less than that of Abu Lahab as they constantly looked for opportunity to give the Prophet hard time.

One day, as the Prophet performed his Prayer, one of them came and threw sheep droppings on him. On another occasion, one of them

---

[163] Ibn Ishaq, *Sirat Rasul Allah*, 2/135
[164] Ibn Hisham, *As-Sirah*, 2/101

filled his bowl which he used for ablution, with filth. After awhile, in order to protect himself from their evil, the noble Prophet constructed a wall between his house and theirs. However, they continued to behave in an ugly manner. One day, the noble Prophet picked up the filth they had thrown into his house with a stick and came out of his house. Then he shouted: "O the sons of Abdulmanaf! What kind of neighborliness is this?"[165]

Uqba ibn Abu Muayt took the matter a bit further and one night when Abu Jahl came to visit him, they sat together at home with a group of friends and made plans to insult the Prophet. As they spoke amongst each other, Abu Jahl pointed to the Prophet and said: "Who amongst you has the courage to throw the intestines of a slaughtered camel down Muhammad's head when he goes down to the prostration position?"

At this point one of them stood up and this person was no other than Uqba. He went and picked up the intestines mentioned before and waited for the right moment. As the noble Prophet went down to the prostration position, he walked towards him and placed the filth on his back. The beloved servant of God was insulted by his neighbors at a point where he was closest to God hence he could not lift his head for some time. Meanwhile, Uqba was proud of what he had done as he and the others laughed and scratched their bellies. That day, they had laughed so much that they leaned on each other in order to stand up. Eventually, Fatimah saw her father and came running to him. She began to remove the filth from her father's back as she had a go at those who were laughing.[166]

Indeed, we can provide many examples such as the one above. The life of the noble Prophet and the Companions who followed was full of incidents like the one where he was harassed with filth. The noble Prophet and his beloved Companions are our guides. A person of service should never lose hope due to the negative incidents that occur

---

[165] Halabi, *Sirah*, 1/474
[166] Ayni, *Umdatu'l-Qari*, 7/26

around him, just as the Prophet, he should continue to serve with patience, perseverance, determination and willpower.

READING TEXT

The New Man

"The cycles of history have brought us to the threshold of a new age, one that is open to the manifestations of God's providence. In the Muslim world, the recent centuries have been characterized by alienation, by the unconscious striving after intellectual fantasies, by opposition to traditional values, the denial of self identity, and confusion. But signs emerging all around us suggest that the twenty first century will be a time of faith, the age of our renaissance.

From out of the fickle crowds of our time, a truly new man will appear: a man, who thinks, reflects, and puts trust in both reason and inspiration. He will pursue perfection in all aspects of life, committing himself to comprehensive and holistic ideals. He will fly balanced on the wings of this world and the next in a successful marriage of heart and mind. Surely, the birth of this new man will not be easy, for pains and travails attend every birth. But when the time comes, a radiant new generation will suddenly be born among us. Like the rain that pours mercifully from dark and heavy clouds, or the waters that well up from the depths of the earth, or the blooms that burst forth as the snow blanket melts, these new men and women will surely come.

The new man will be full of integrity, determined to maintain his unique identity against all improper influences. Nothing will be able to limit his vision and movement, and no foreign ideologies will distract him from his spiritual path. His thought, his will, and his imagination will be completely free. He will be free in all things because he will serve only God, rejecting the slavish emulation of others and forging his own identity through his commitment to traditional virtues.

The new person will search, reflect, and believe. He will value spirituality and be filled with spiritual pleasures. In establishing his own identity, he will demonstrate his distinctiveness by subordinating the technological means of his time to the perennial values of his tradition. He will be inspired by the lofty personalities that constitute his glorious heritage, and configure his beliefs and thoughts accordingly. He will enthusiastically practice his values everywhere, never abandoning contemplation. Instead, he will passionately dedicate his life to the establishment of truth. Without concern for felicity and prosperity, he will readily give up everything he possesses for the sake of this cause. Like one who sows seeds in the bosom of the earth, he will pour out everything he has been given for the sake of his people and actively anticipate their future prosperity.

The new person will be part of the new generation and will utilize all possible means for reaching the minds and hearts of people, from publication to mass media. This generation of new men and women will represent their values everywhere and restore international dignity to their people. Although deeply spiritual, these new men and women will engage with all aspects of the modern world. This generation will demonstrate mastery in all human endeavors, from science to the arts, from technology to metaphysics. Their love of knowledge will be insatiable, their passion for wisdom will be renewed every day, and their spiritual depths will be beyond imagination. They will be like the enlightened people of the past, competing with the angels as they ascend toward God.

The new man will be filled with love for all creation. He will guard the human virtues, seek guidance from the moral principles that make us human, and find himself in them. He will be so universal that he will embrace the whole of existence with compassion. The new man chooses his way of life and seeks to shape society accordingly. He will protect what is good in his community and encourages others to do so. He will struggle vigilantly against evil until the day it is removed from society. He will encourage everyone toward faith and promote education. To him, service to God is beautiful, and he will practice it fully. He will support the social services that respect spiritual values and engage fully with public life. He will always advocate for the people and will bear the mark of responsibility among his community.

The new man will be filled with the creative spirit, despising formalism and clichés. He will find renewal in a return to his essential humanity. He will take responsibility for the course of time and walk ahead of his era, looking always toward the future. He will work with supernatural effort and yet rely absolutely on the strength of God. He will be so vigilant in his obedience to the laws of nature and to the will of God that the ignorant might mistake him for a naturalist or a fatalist. But he will always be a man of balance, observing the laws of causality and submitting to God, as his faith requires.

The new man will be a conqueror and a discoverer: Every day, he will carry his flag deeper into his soul and further toward the immensities of the universe, charging the gates of both the inner and outer worlds. His faith and wisdom will give him the confidence to approach the metaphysical reality beneath phenomena, and he will establish his headquarters in the realms beyond. Finally, when the grave calls him and he goes to receive his bounties, the heavens will not hesitate to welcome him."[167]

QUESTIONS

1- Who is the Companion who made the following statement when he was about to be executed? "By God no! Have you seen a sign of betrayal on me? Executing him in my place to safe my own life aside, I would rather be executed even to protect him from a thorn that may pierce his noble foot."

   a. Hubayb

   b. Khalid

   c. Talha

   d. Ubaydullah

2- To whom, did the Prophet make the following statement? "My dear uncle! By God, in order to change my mind, even if they placed the sun in one of my hands and the moon in other, I will not be discouraged and I will continue on this path until God grants me victory!"

   a. Abu Lahab

   b. Abu Talib

---

[167] Gülen, M. Fethullah, "Yeni İnsan," *Sızıntı*, issue 146, March 1991

    c. Abu Jahl

    d. Ibn Abbas

3- Which of the below fills the gap in the following sentence: "Perseverance and determination are nourished from ...."

    a. body

    b. data

    c. carnal soul

    d. faith

4- To whom, did the Prophet gave the following advice? "Control and renew your ship one more time because the ocean is deep. Make sure you take sufficient rations, without doubt, the journey is long. Your load should be light because the hills which you shall climb are steep. Be sincere in your deeds because our Lord, Who is All-Seeing and All-Hearing, knows about everything you do."

    a. Abu Dharr

    b. Mus'ab

    c. Bilal

    d. Zayd

5- Which of the below fills the gap in the following verse? *"Alif. Lam. Mim. Do people reckon that they will be left (to themselves at ease) on their mere saying, '...................,' and will not be put to a test? We certainly tested those who preceded them. (This is Our unchanging way) so that God will certainly mark out those who prove true (in their profession of faith), and He will certainly mark out those who prove false."*

    a. Forgive our sins

    b. We believe

    c. We obey

    d. O God, forgive us

ANSWER KEY

1. The Sentiment of Responsibility and Serving Religion
   1. A 2. C 3. D 4. B 5. C 6. A 7. B 8. D 9. B 10. A
2. Striving in God's Cause, Invitation and Guidance
   1. C 2. B 3. D 4. C 5. A 6. D 7. A 8. A 9. C 10. D
3. Representation: The Tongue of Conduct
   1. B 2. C 3. A 4. C 5. A
4. *Ukhuwah*: Brotherhood
   1. A 2. C 3. D 4. A 5. B 6. A 7. C 8. A
5. Altruism and Munificence
   1. B 2. C 3. B 4. A 5. D 6. B 7. B 8. D 9. A 10. C
6. Consultation (*Istisharah*)
   1. D 2. C 3. D 4. C 5. A 6. A 7. B
7. Love, Passion, and Renewing One's Self / 8. Perseverance and Determination
   1. A 2. B 3. D 4. A 5. B